I0484923

Owen Sound Ontario Book 1 in Colour Photos, Saving Our History One Photo at a Time

Photography
by Barbara Raué
2014

Series Name:
Cruising Ontario

Book 92: Owen Sound

Cover photo: Golden Grain Elevators at sunset

Series Name: Cruising Ontario
Saving Our History One Photo at a Time
in colour photos

Other Books by Barbara Raue

Coins of Gold

Arrows, Indians and Love

The Life and Times of Barbara
Volume 1: Inventions That Have Enhanced My Life
Volume 2: Entertainment That I Have Enjoyed
Volume 3: East Coast Trips
Volume 4: Olympics Have Always Intrigued Me
Volume 5: Wonders of the World
Volume 6: Caribbean Cruises We Have Enjoyed
Volume 7: Animals
Volume 8: Storms and Other Major Disasters in My Lifetime
Volume 9: Wars, Terrorist Attacks and Major Disasters

The Cromwell Family Book

Laura Secord Discovered

Visit Barbara's website to view all of her books
http://barbararaue.ca

Owen Sound is located on the southern shores of Georgian Bay in a valley below the sheer rock cliffs of the Niagara Escarpment. The city is located at the mouths of the Pottawatomi and Sydenham Rivers. It has tree-lined streets, many parks, and tree-covered hillsides and ravines.

This area of the upper Great Lakes was first surveyed in 1815 by William Fitzwilliam Owen and Lieutenant Henry W. Bayfield. The inlet was named "Owen's Sound" in honour of the explorer's older brother, Admiral Sir Edward Owen.

The city was first known as Sydenham when it was settled in 1840 by Charles Rankin. Prior to his arrival, the area was inhabited by the Ojibway people. In 1857 the name was changed to Owen Sound. For much of its history, it was a major port city known as the "Chicago of the North."

The Old Mail Road was the first into the County, running from Barrie to Meaford. The Toronto-Sydenham Road (Highway 10) was constructed in 1848. In 1868 the first telegraphy system was established connecting the County with Toronto.

The Tom Thomson Memorial Art Gallery is located in Owen Sound. Tom Thomson was born in 1877 and grew up in a home that appreciated literature and music. He worked as an engraver. In 1912, he sketched in Algonquin Park and canoed the Spanish River. The result was a full size canvas, Northern Lake. He returned each year to Algonquin Park where he supported himself as a ranger and guide as he continued to paint, producing masterpieces such as Autumn Foliage, The West Wind, and Northern River.

William Avery "Billy" Bishop was born in Owen Sound in 1894. Given a .22 rifle one Christmas, Billy was offered 25 cents for every squirrel he shot. "One bullet – one shot" became Billy's motto. Bishop flew planes in the First World War. Courage and marksmanship made him one of the war's greatest fighter pilots.

Norman Bethune was born in 1890 in Gravenhurst. From childhood he dreamed of becoming a doctor like his paternal grandfather, one of the founders of the University of Toronto's Medical School. The family moved to Owen Sound where Norman finished high school. In 1914, one year short of finishing his medical training, he left for France as a stretcher bearer, Navy surgeon, and as a senior medical officer in the new Royal Canadian Air Force. After returning home to Canada, he was appointed to the McGill University teaching staff where, as a thoracic surgeon he invented new surgical instruments. He supported a universal health insurance plan for Canadians. While in Spain during the Spanish Civil War, he organized a mobile blood transfusion service, the first of its kind. In 1938, Bethune went to China to work in Mao Tse-Tung's 8th route army, performing surgical operations in field hospitals. He cut his hand and it became infected and led to his death in 1939. The Gravenhust home where he was born has been restored as the Bethune Memorial Home.

Agnes Campbell Macphail was born in 1890 in Grey County. In 1921, she became the first woman to be elected to the Canadian parliament. She was later elected to the Ontario Legislature where she was responsible for the province's first equal pay legislation.

The Propeller Capital of Canada

William Kennedy, a mill-wright's apprentice from Glasgow, Scotland, sailed for Canada in 1831, settling first at Smith's Falls. In 1856 he arrived in Sydenham (Owen Sound) to install machinery in Harrison's wool and grist mills. He remained in the village establishing his own planning and matching mills in 1857.

In 1863 Kennedy built a large two-storey building on the west shore of the harbor. The Port of Owen Sound was expanding rapidly and Kennedy quickly realized the opportunities there were for the manufacture of equipment for fishing, passenger, freight and pleasure boats. He also made machinery for saw, grist and flour mills, and, in later years, for cement mills.

William Kennedy died in 1885 and was succeeded by his son, Matthew, who put a steel foundry into operation in 1899. By 1911 William Kennedy and Sons Ltd. employed 150 people, manufacturing turbines, mill gearings, steel castings and propellers.

During World War I, the company purchased the Owen Sound Iron Works and the Canadian Malleable Iron Work. After surviving the Great Depression, Kennedy's foundry supplied the propellers for all ships built in Canada during the World War II ship building program – fighting craft as well as merchant vessels. Canadian propellers ranged in size from a few kilograms to powerful 15 tonne screws for Canada's largest fighting craft.

For almost half a century, the Kennedy whistle called its employees to work, announced the lunch hour and signaled when to put down their tools at day's end. Kennedy's whistle was so accurate you could set your watch by it. Initially activated by steam, its sound was heard at seven a.m., noon, one and five o'clock. After the factory closed in 1997, the whistle fell silent. In 2002 the whistle was installed and made operational at the Owen Sound Marine and Rail Museum. It sounds its whistle Monday through Saturday at noon and five o'clock.

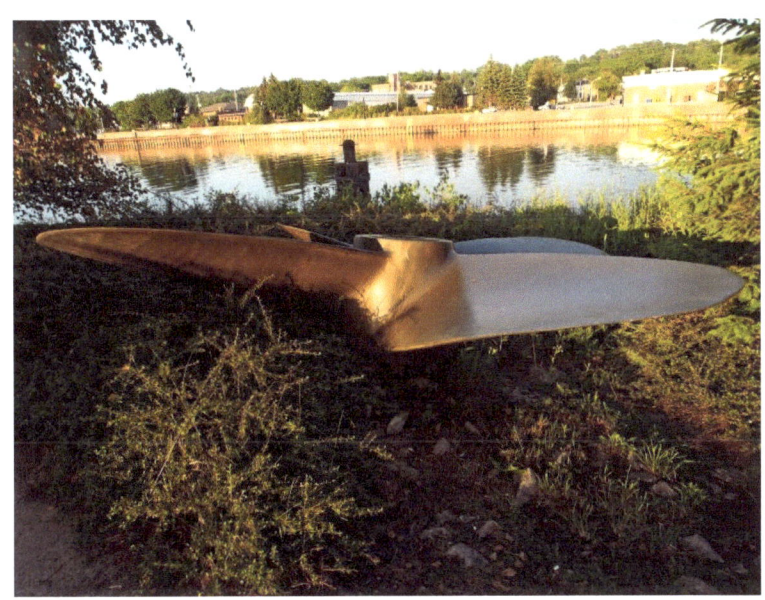

Propeller

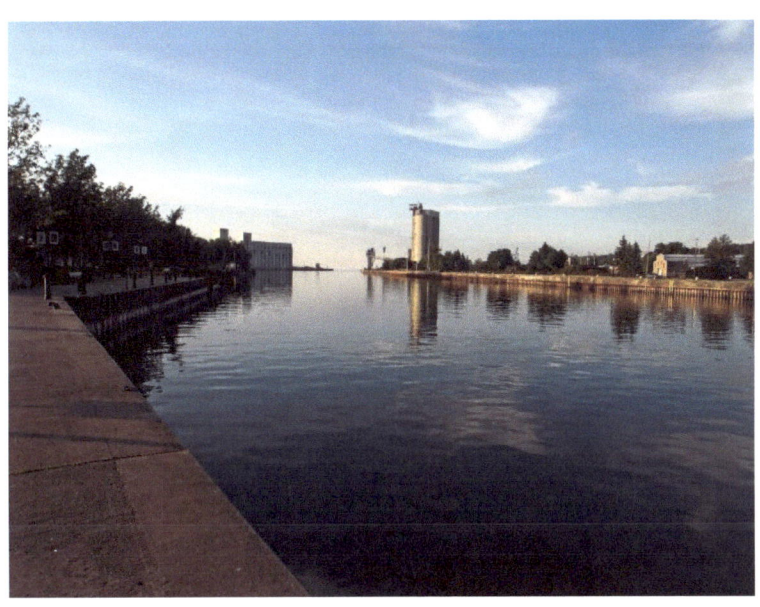

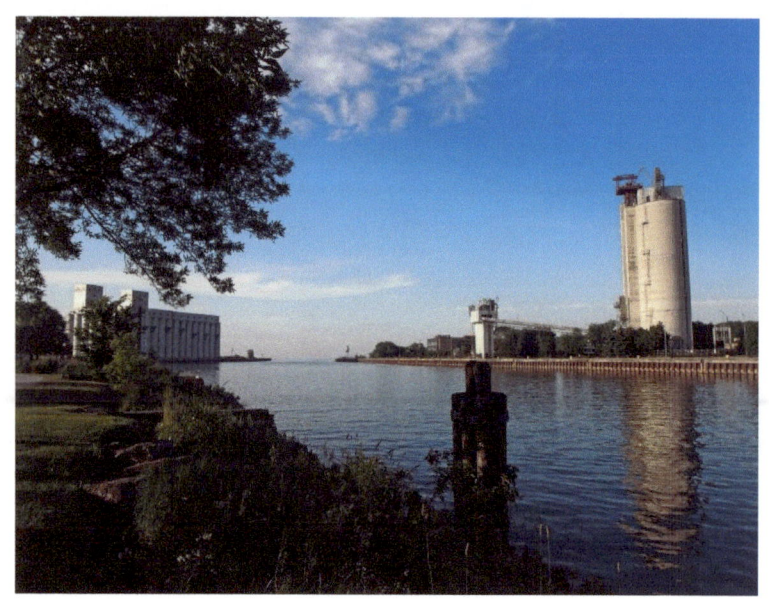

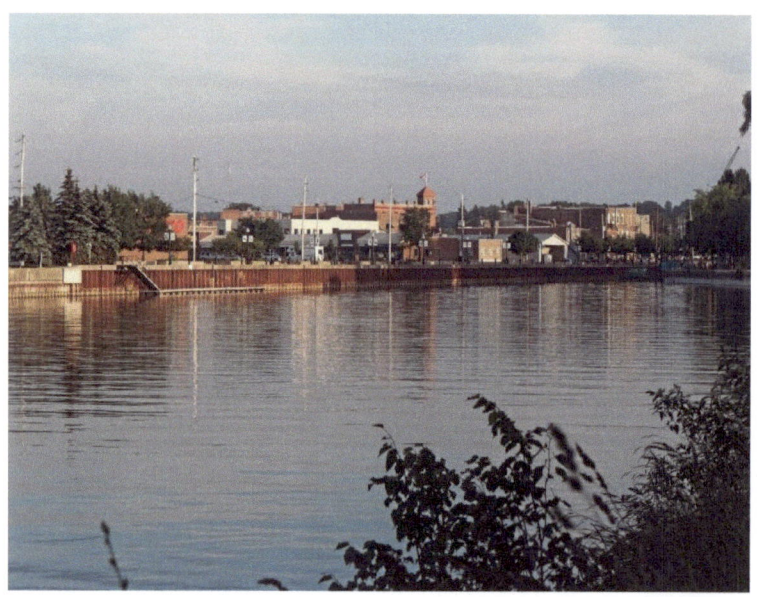

The launch of the steamship City of Owen Sound by Captain John Simpson in 1875 so impressed the townsmen John Harrison, John Corbet and William Kough, that they established the Owen Sound Dry Dock Shipbuilding and Navigation Company later that year; this was the first Canadian Dry Dock on the Upper Lakes. The company employed hundreds of craftsmen and turned out many of the famous Great Lakes wooden steamships. Over the next thirty years Owen Sound's shipbuilders launched over 100 vessels and repaired hundreds more. Their success was an important factor in the material prosperity of the town.

In the history of the Great Lakes maritime industry there are few instances where a sailor became a ship owner and founder of a fleet of lake vessels. George Hindman rose from wheelsman to captain to the owner of the Hindman Transportation Company, a fleet of seven ships that transported grain, coal, iron ore and pulpwood.

Hindman invested in Manitoulin Island timber and became a ship owner in 1930. The Hindman Transportation Company, which never lost a ship due to sinking, grounding or collision, became the longest-lived privately owned Great Lakes Shipbuilding company in history. Captain Hindman named his vessels after members of his family.

Owen Sound Coat of Arms

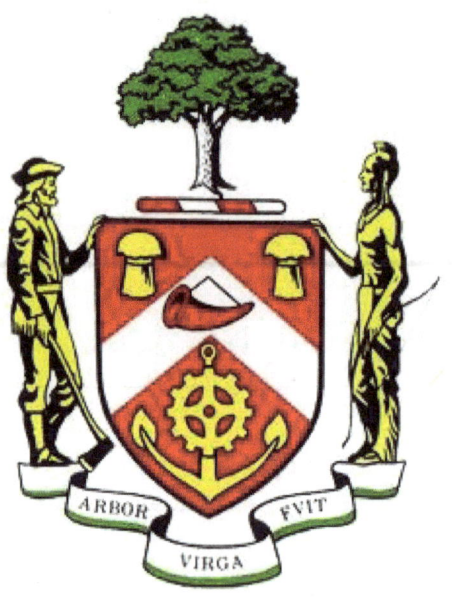

At the top of the shield on a red background (signifying courage) are two golden sheaves of wheat that represent the agricultural economy of both the early settlers and the present day. At the bottom of the shield is a geared wheel to show the industrial nature of the community. It is placed over an anchor to suggest the marine economy. The spokes of the wheel form a quatrefoil interpreted as a four bladed propeller.

The place of importance on the shield is reserved for the horn, which according to local history, was blown by John Telfer, the first citizen, to attract the attention of Charles Rankin, the government surveyor, who was in the bush nearby. The shield is supported on the right by a pioneer who, dressed in the costume of the early 1800s, rests an axe near his feet; the axe signifies the labour in clearing the site for homesteads.

The Native person wears the headdress of the earliest known tribe in the valley; because of the custom of tying their hair in a lock at the crown of the head, Champlain and the French explorers called these people "high hairs". He carries a bow to indicate a hunting economy.

The ribbon bears the Latin motto "arbor virga fuit" which means "as the twig is bent so grows the tree".

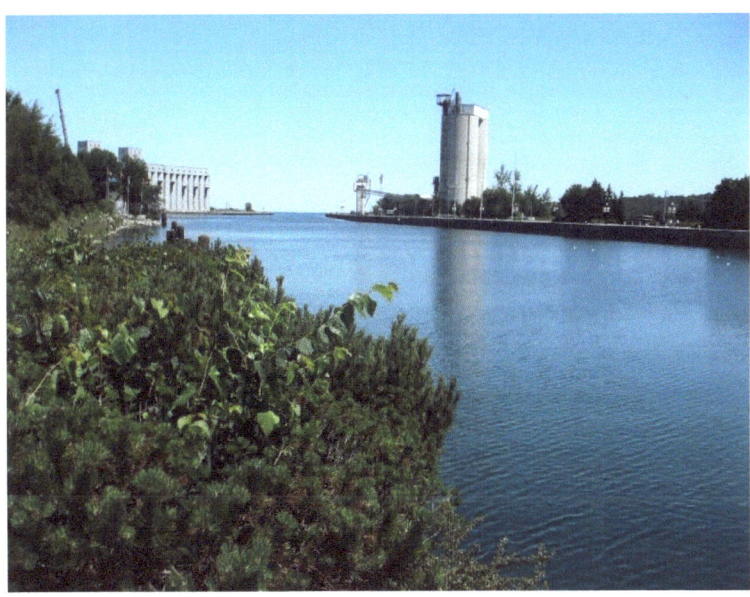

From 1885 to 1912 the Canadian Pacific Railway made the Port of Owen Sound the eastern terminus of their steamship line. Thousands of immigrants moved through this "Gateway to the West" while millions of bushels of prairie grain were transported east.

As settlements accelerated in western Canada, Owen Sound became the busiest port on the Upper Great Lakes and earned the nickname "Chicago of the North."

Three Scottish built steamers, 80 metres long, left Owen Sound three times a week. The Alberta, Athabasca and Algoma completed the run to Port Arthur (Thunder Bay) in less than two days, shortening travel time from Toronto to Winnipeg to an unprecedented 65 hours.

When the Algoma wrecked on Isle Royale in Lake Superior in 1885, the CPR commissioned a successor. The S.S. Manitoba, Canada's first all steel steamer, was launched in 1889 by the Polson Iron Works Company from their shipyard on the east shore of Owen Sound's harbor. Two additional steamers, the Assiniboia and he Keewatin, joined the CPR fleet in 1907.

Disaster struck in 1911 when the grain elevators burned to the ground. The fire, along with the difficult terrain and steep grades between Owen Sound and Toronto, convinced the CPR to establish its own harbor at Port McNicoll, a place more easily accessible by rail. On May 1, 1912, after 27 years of operating out of Owen Sound, the Canadian Pacific fleet left the city for the last time. As the town's citizens watched, the five vessels sailed away at five minute intervals. The Georgian Bay port was no longer Gateway to the West.

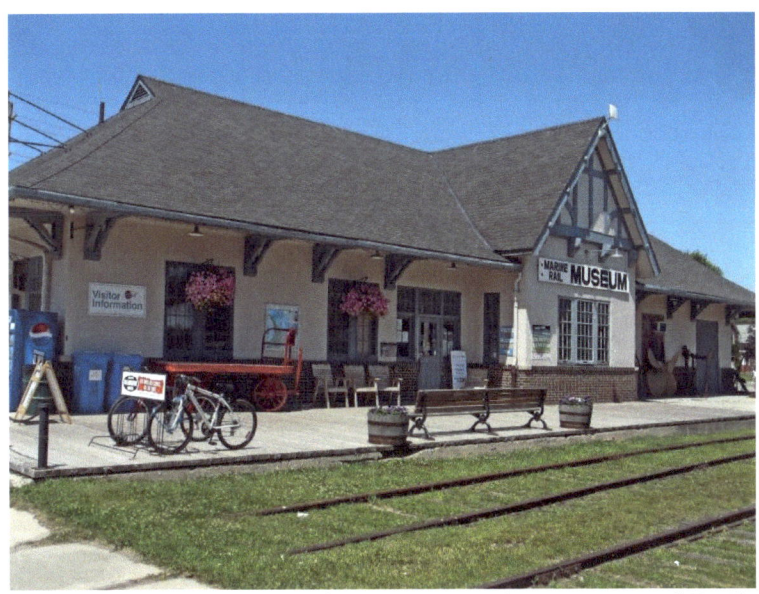

1155 First Avenue West – former Canadian National Railway
Station built in 1932 – passenger service ended in 1970,
freight service in 1986 (tracks removed in 1995)
Now Marine & Rail Museum and Visitor Information Centre

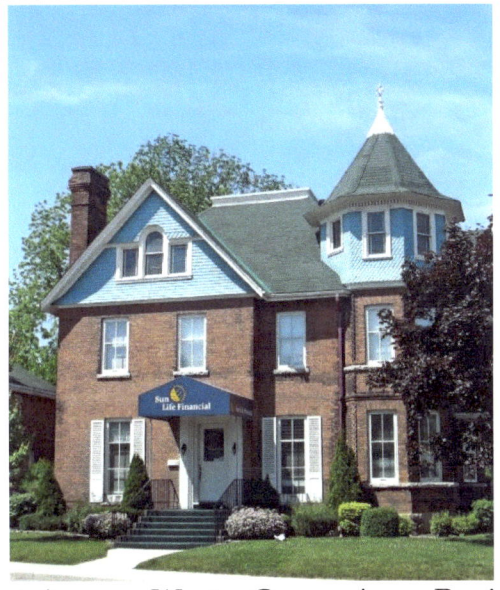

1000 First Avenue West – Queen Anne Revival style
built in 1893-94 – turret, Palladian window

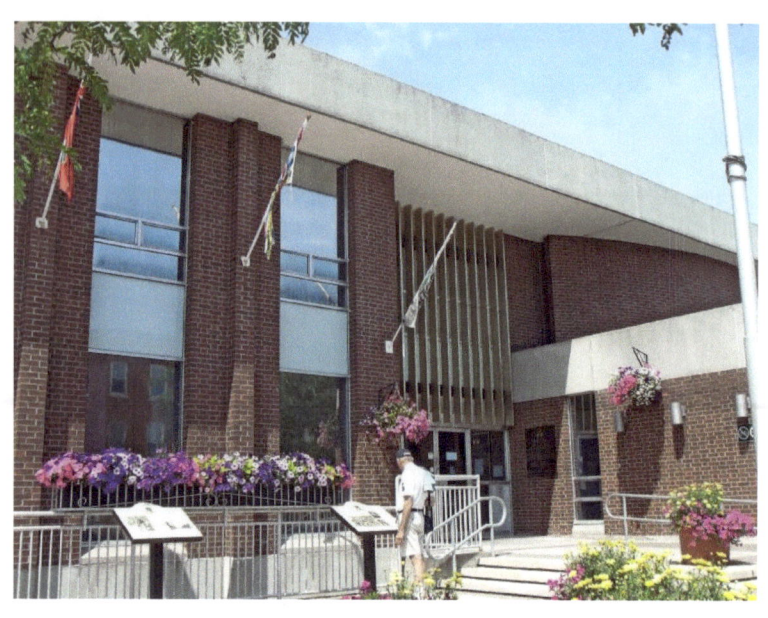

Carnegie Public Library, 1st Avenue West
Built in 1911, opened February 3, 1914

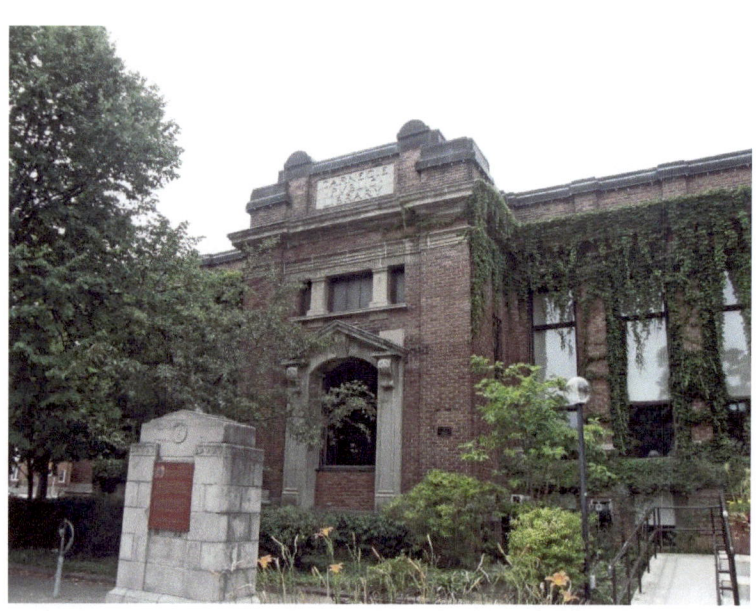

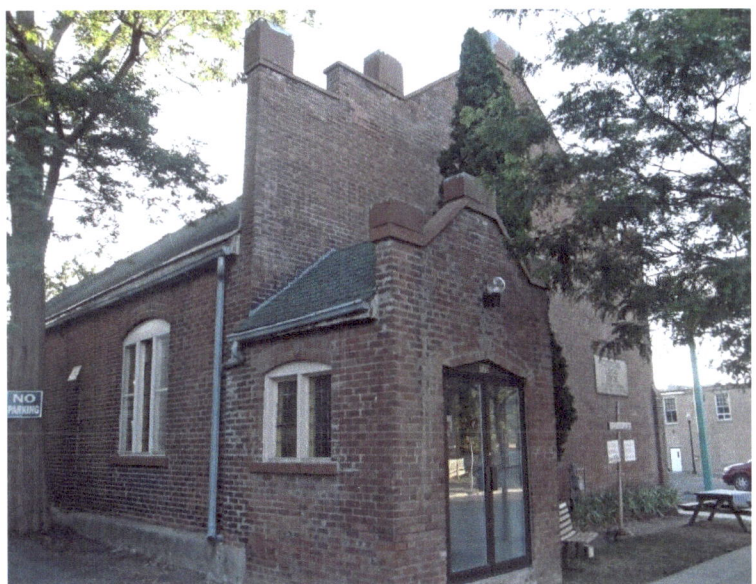

#720

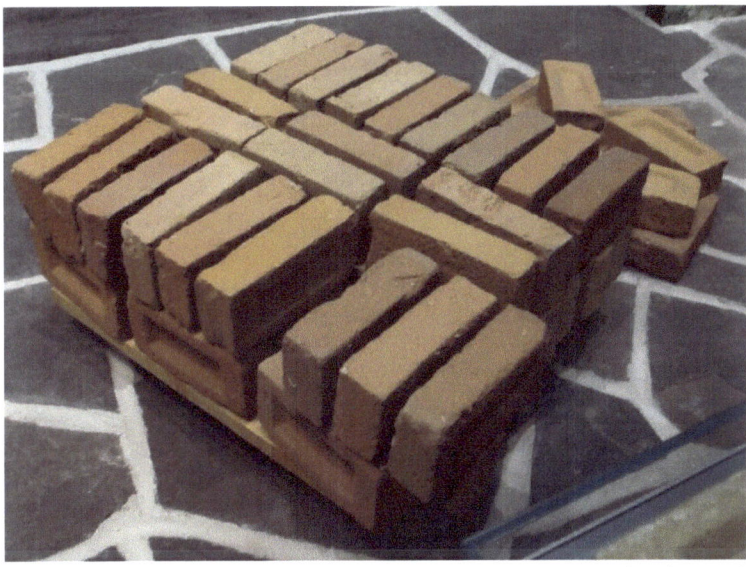

Early Grey County residents made their own bricks from local clay. Red brick is made from clay deposits close to the earth's surface; this clay has a higher iron content. Deeper, lime-rich clays produce buff bricks.

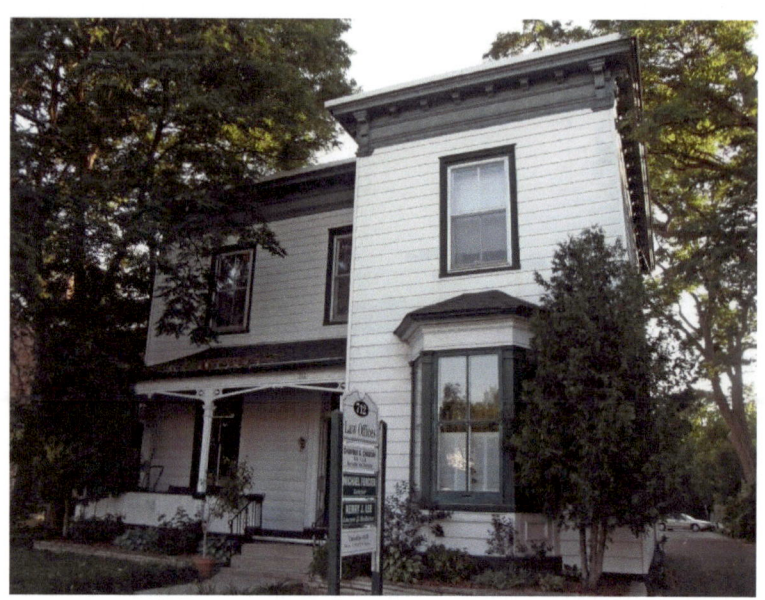

#712 – cornice brackets, bay window

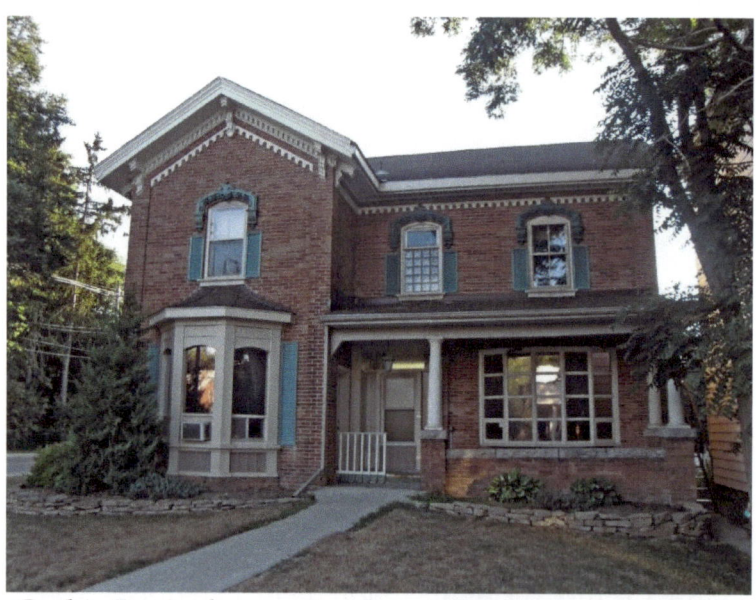

Gothic Revival – cornice decoration, keystones above
windows, bay window

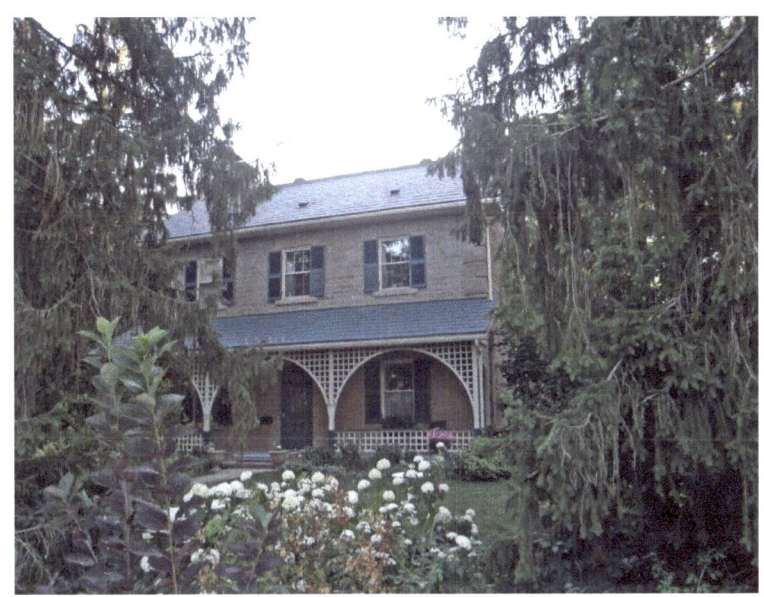

#682

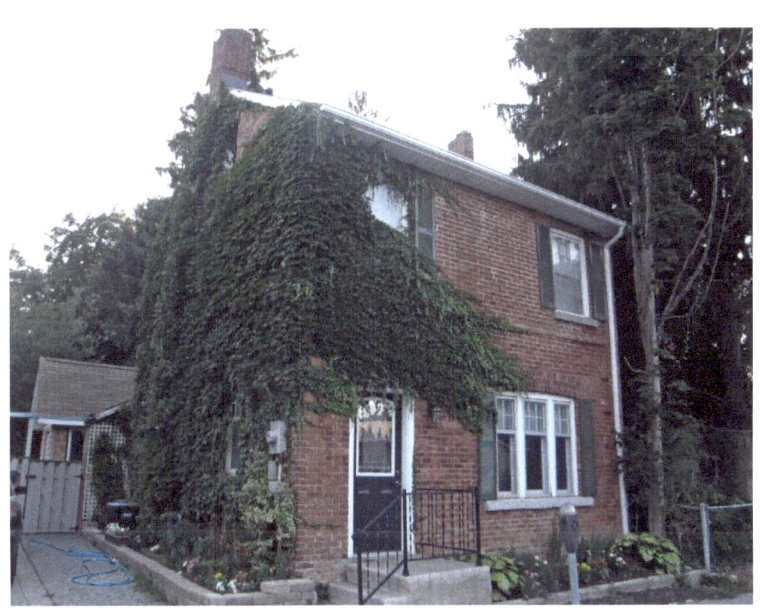

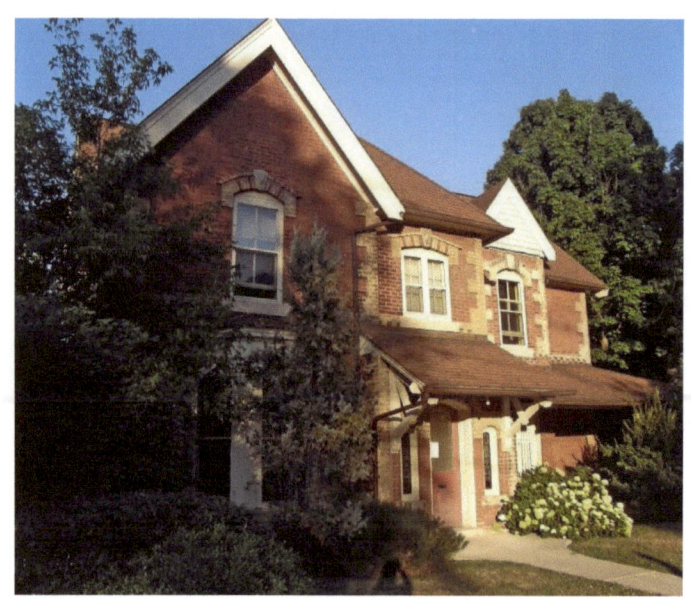

Gothic Revival, corner quoins, dichromatic brick work,
Two-storey frontispiece on right side of building

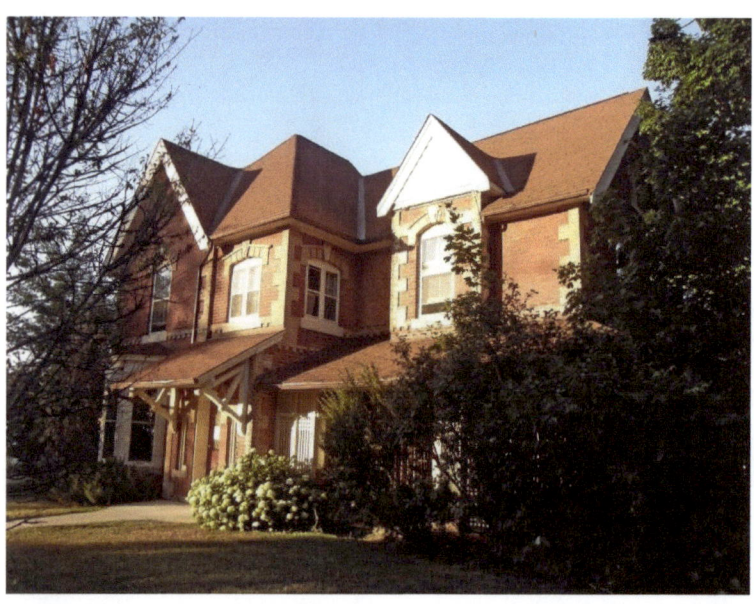

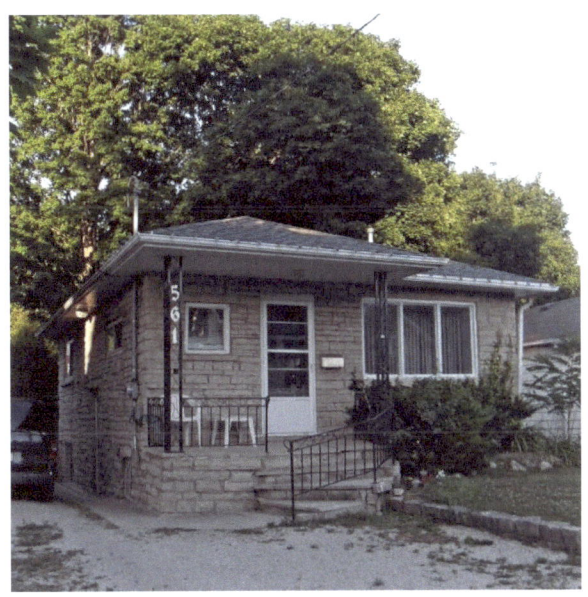

#561 - Regency Cottage

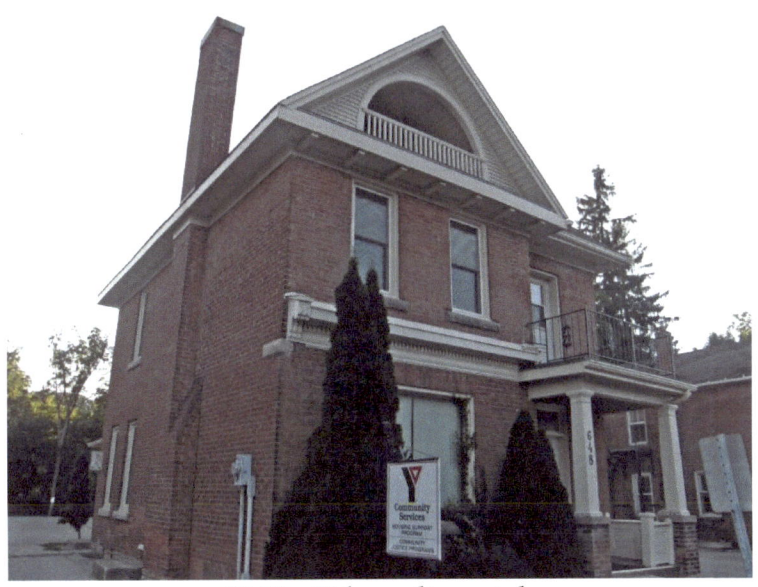

#648 – Edwardian style

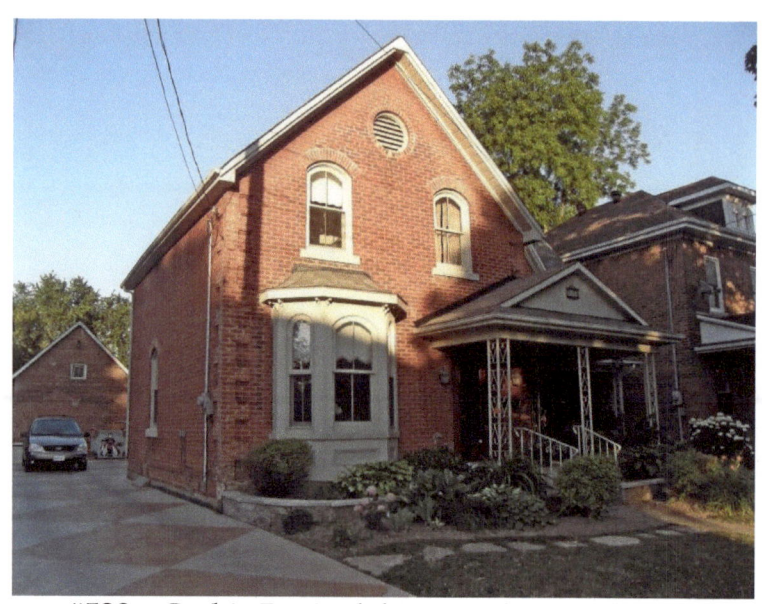

#529 – Gothic Revival, bay window, pediment

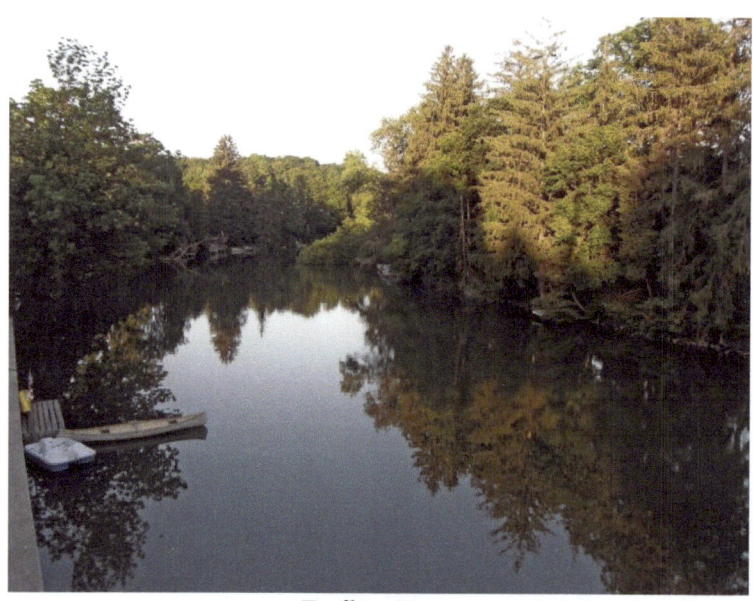

Reflections

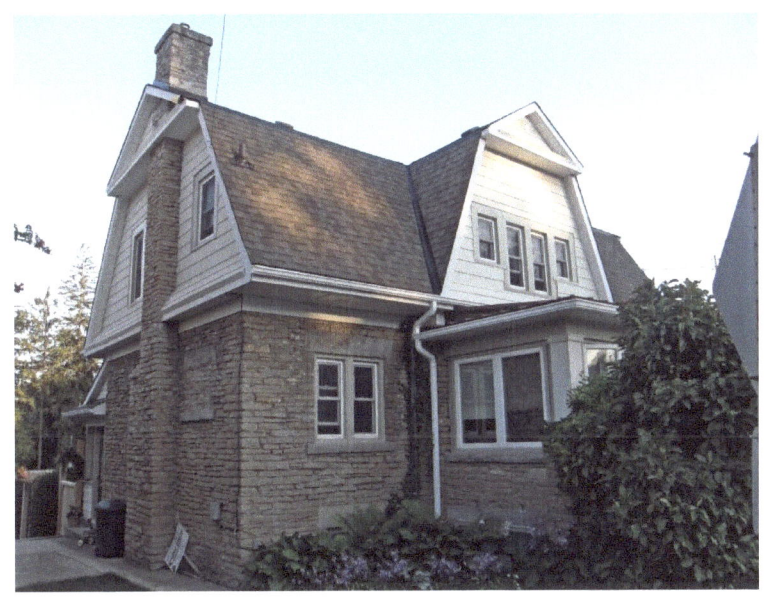

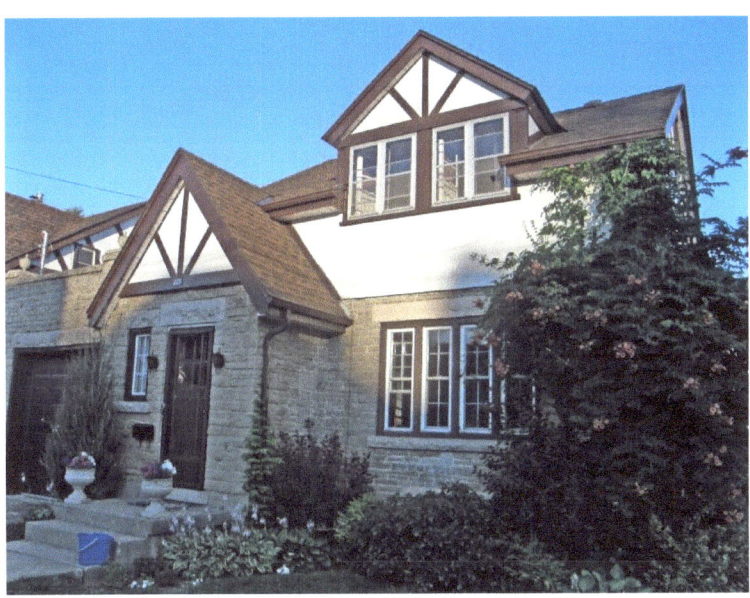

#209 – stone building, Tudor accents

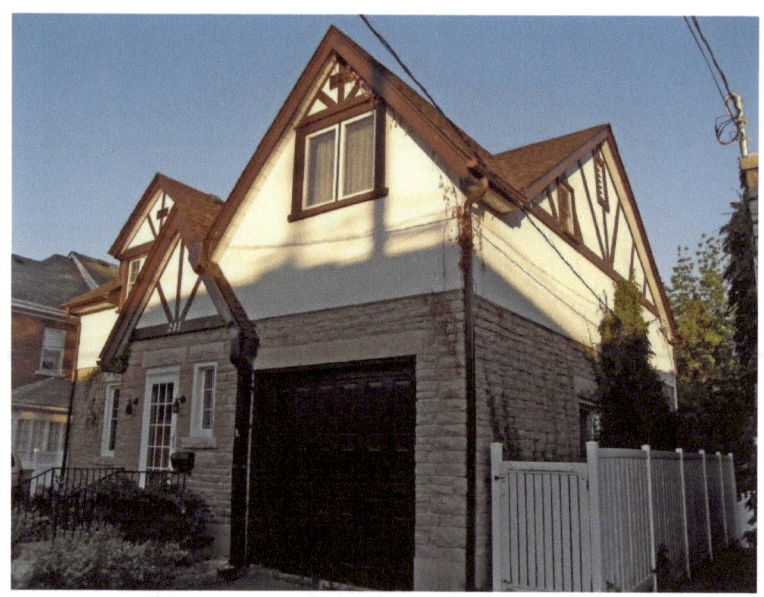

#211 – stone building, Tudor accents

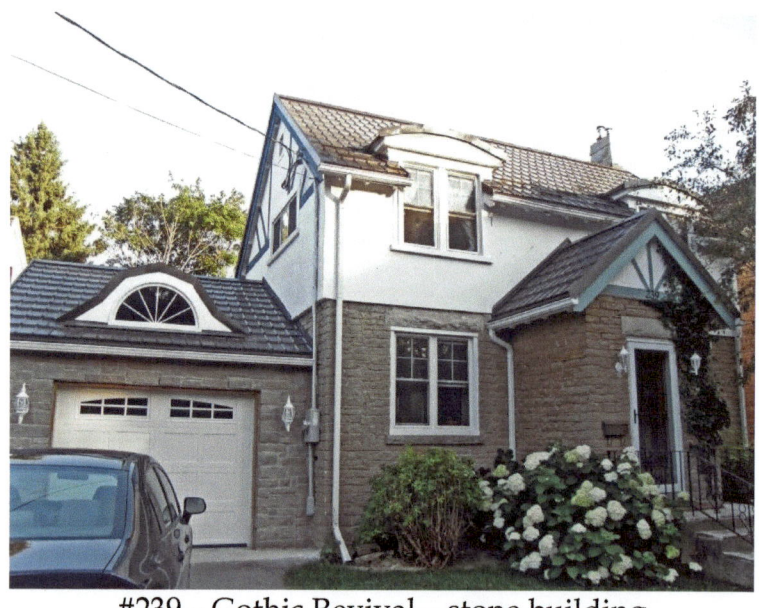

#239 – Gothic Revival – stone building

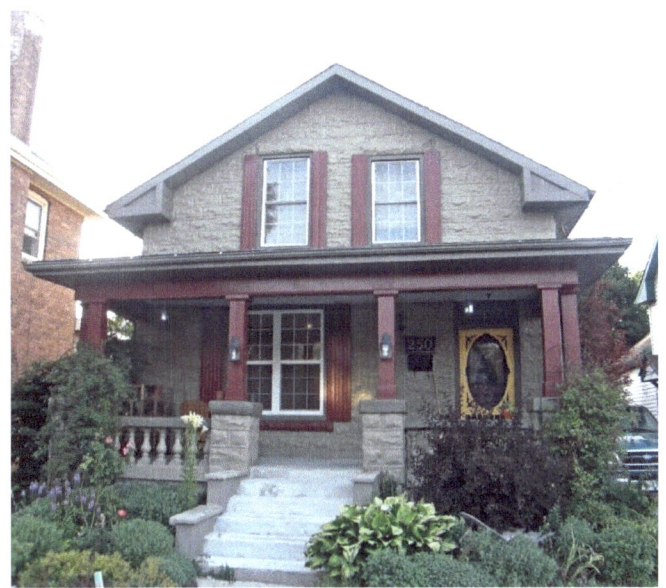

#250 – Gothic Revival

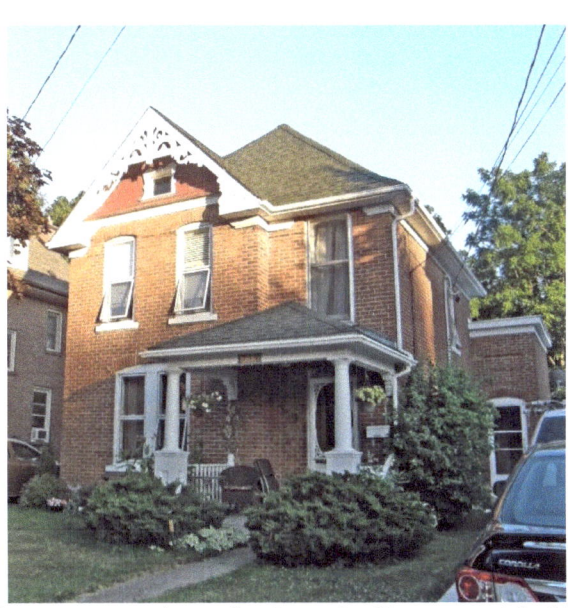

#359 – fancy gingerbread trim – Italianate with 2½ storey
frontispiece, verge board trim on gable

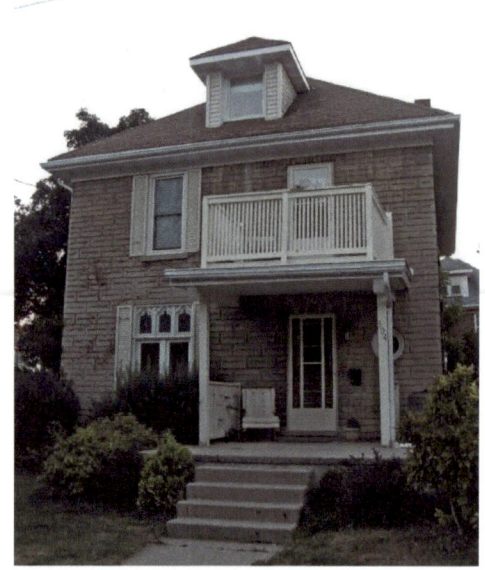

#504 – Italianate, hipped roof, dormer

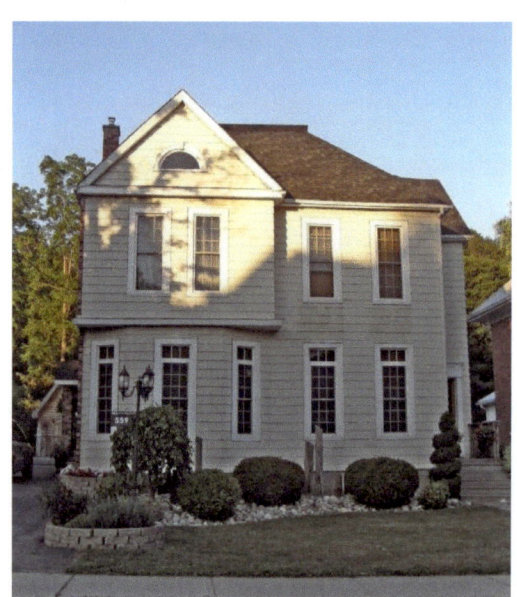

#559

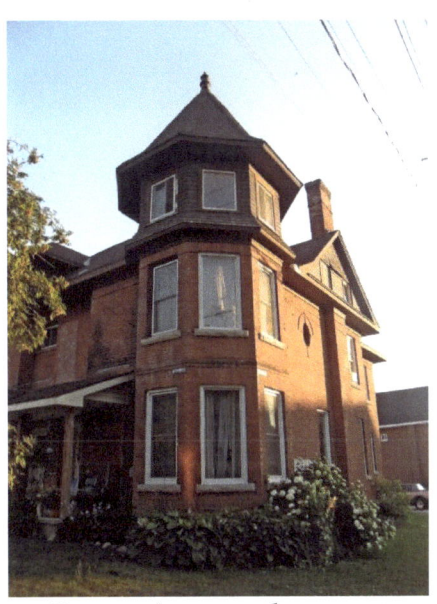

Queen Anne style, turret

Corner of 4th Avenue East and 6th Street East

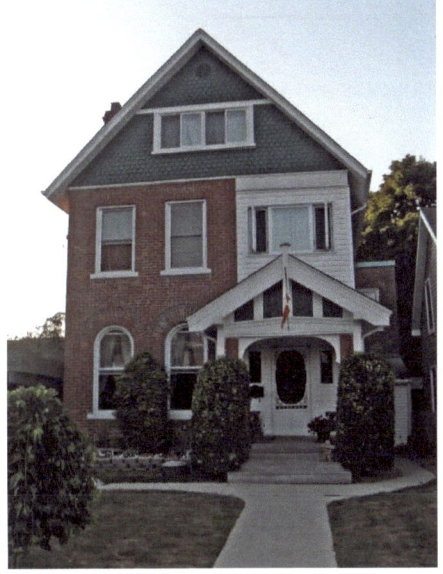

Edwardian style

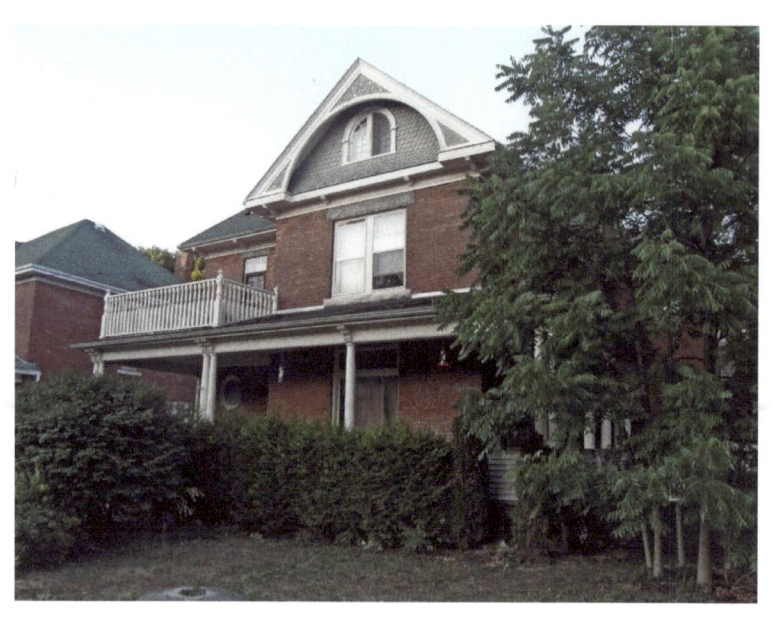

6th Street East and 3rd Avenue

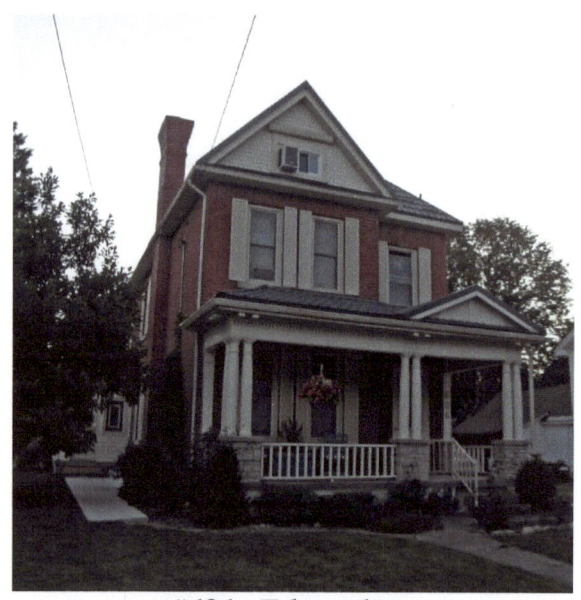

#626 - Edwardian

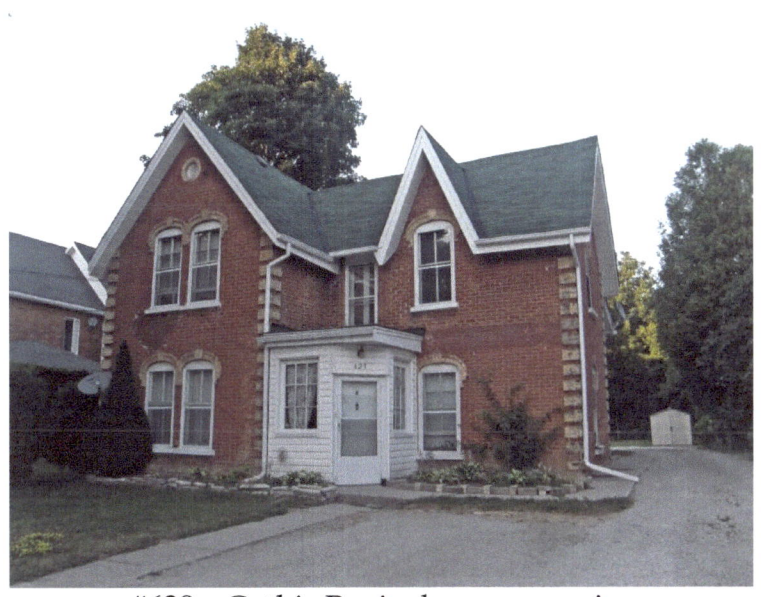

#629 – Gothic Revival, corner quoins

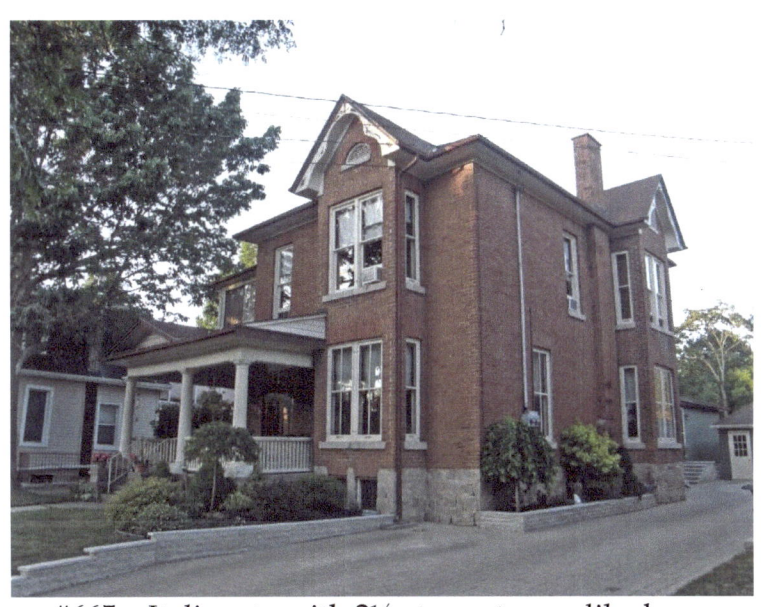

#665 – Italianate with 2½ storey tower-like bays,
verge board trim on gables

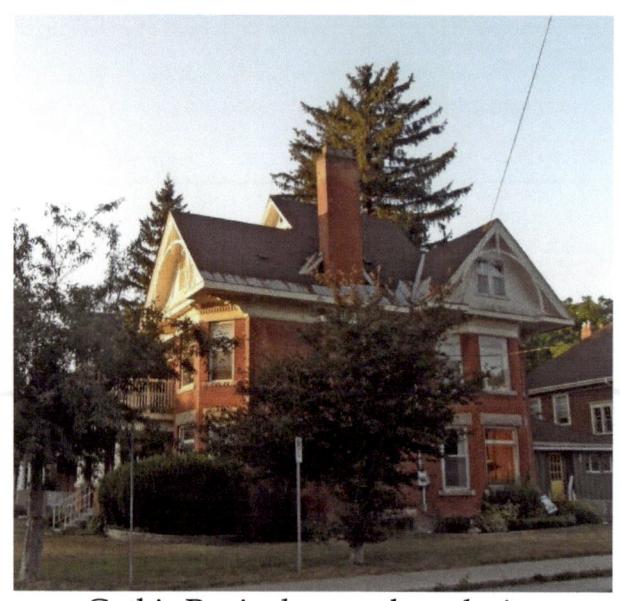

Gothic Revival, verge board trim

7th Street East and 3rd Avenue

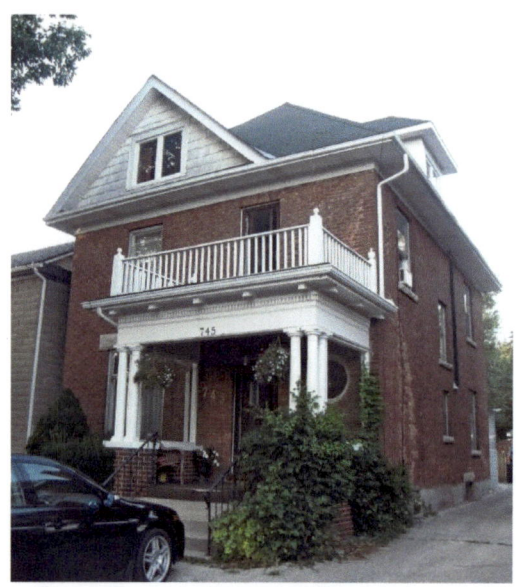

#745 – Italianate – dormers, balcony on second floor

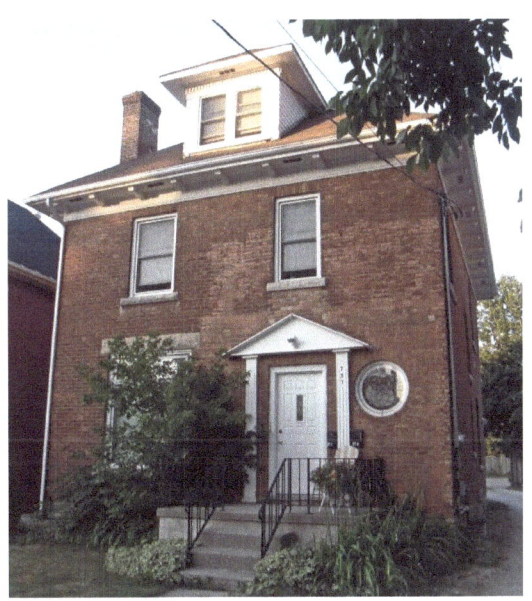

#757 – Italianate, hipped roof, dormer

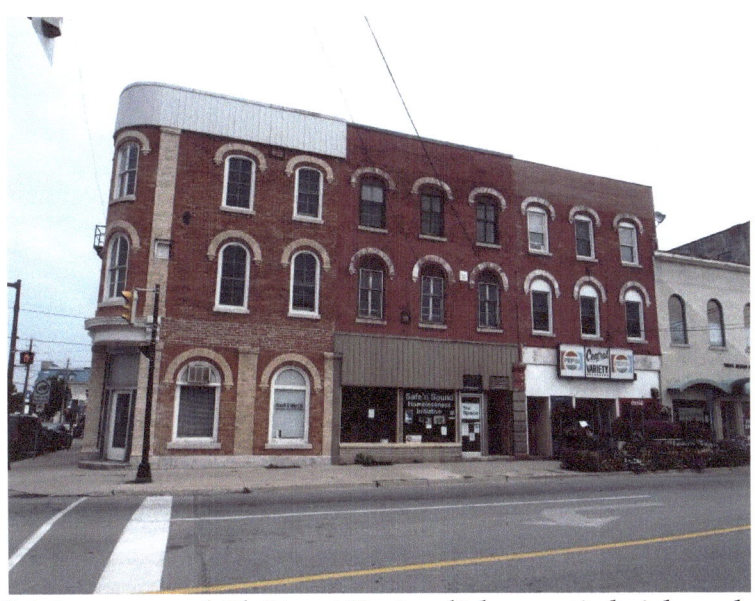

3rd Avenue and 8th Street East – dichromatic brickwork

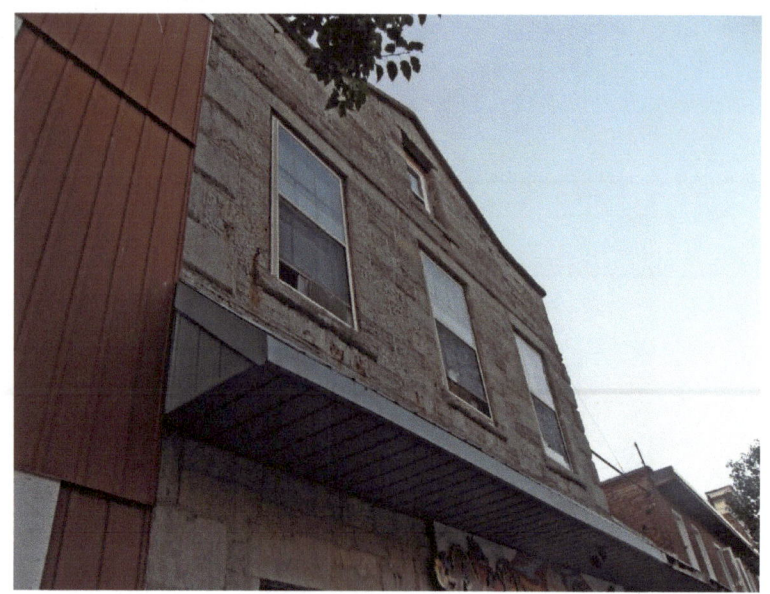

Old stone building

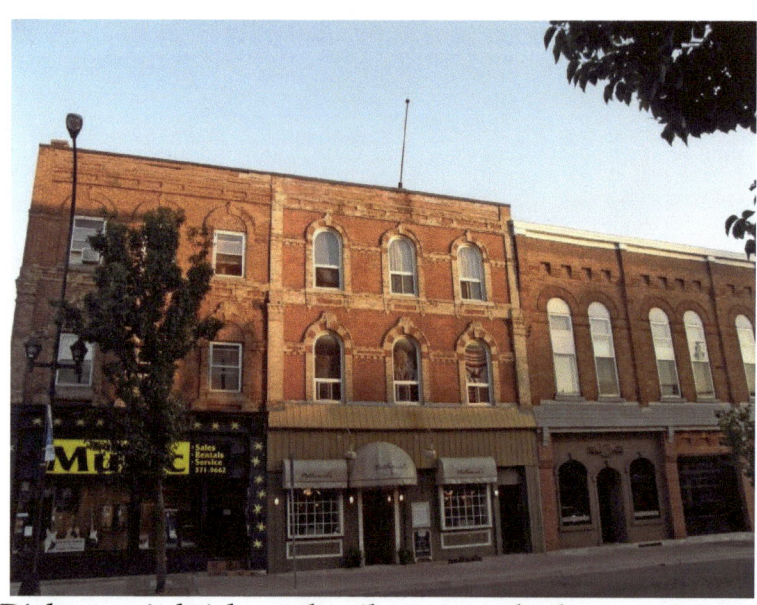

Dichromatic brick work, pilasters, arched voussoirs and keystones, beveled corbels

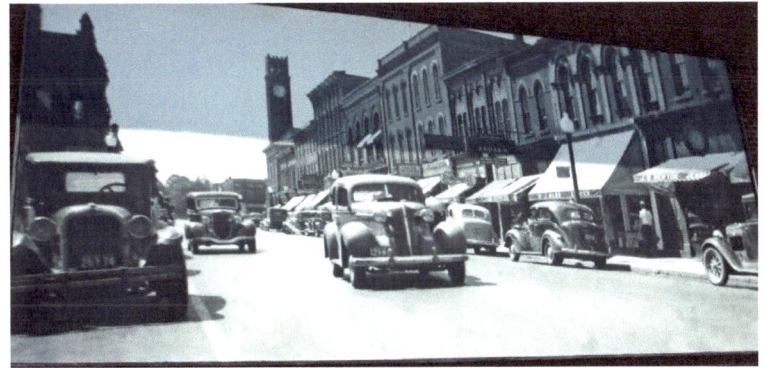

mural

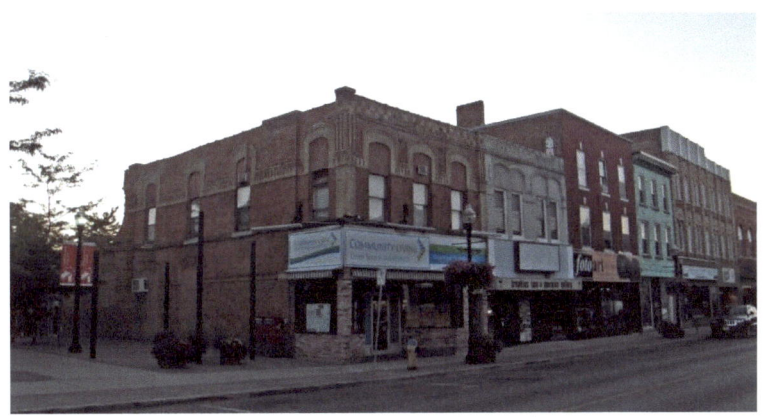

Dichromatic brickwork

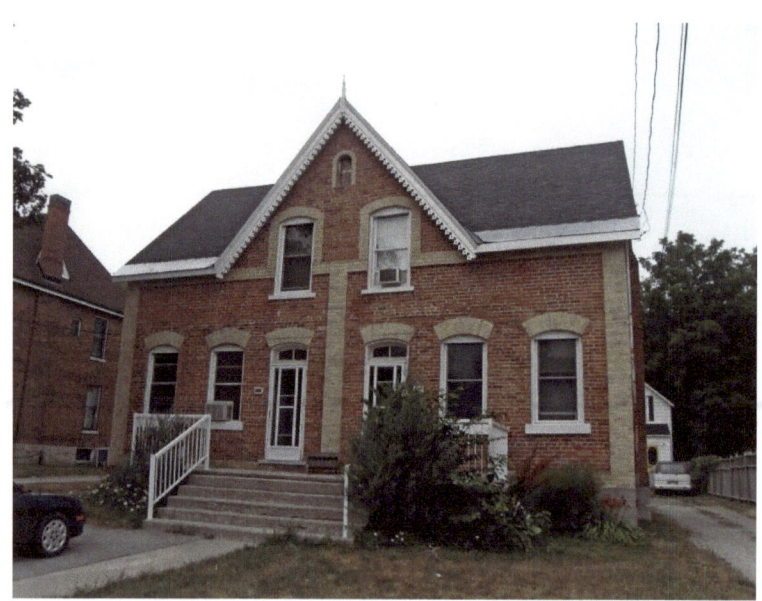

#960 – Gothic Revival – verge board trim and finial

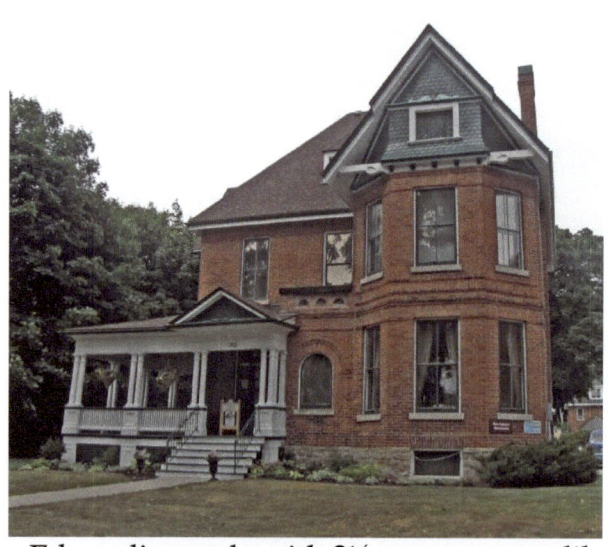

#948 – Edwardian style with 2½ storey tower-like bay,
pediment above verandah

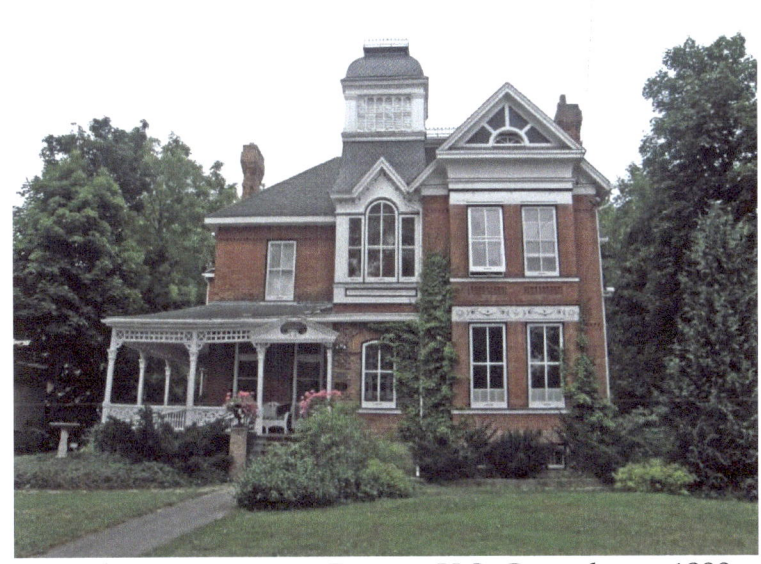

932 3rd Avenue West - Former U.S. Consulate – 1890 –
Vernacular example with Italianate influence, tower

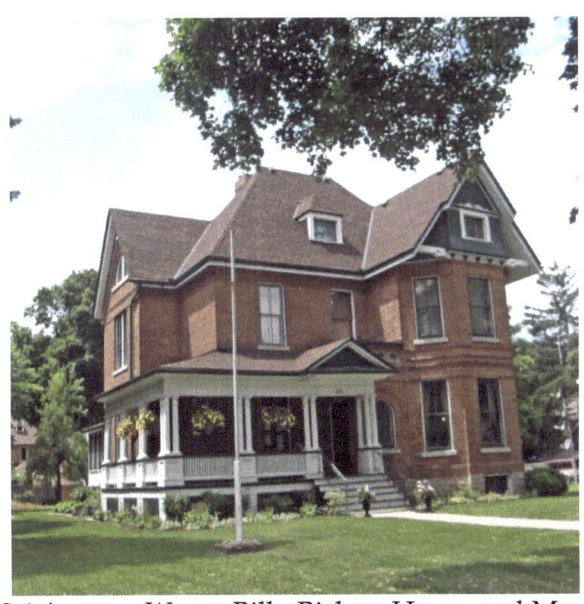

948 3rd Avenue West - Billy Bishop Home and Museum
Built 1884 – Queen Anne Revival style, asymmetrical proportions, a
variety of window shapes and decorative millwork

While not overly extravagant, the Bishop family home is a relatively large estate. The Bishops wished to show their stability while being careful not to flaunt their wealth and thus the lavish details were kept to a minimum. Mrs. Bishop received a sizable inheritance from her family which helped fund the construction of the house, while Mr. Bishop worked from home as a lawyer (his office has since been transformed into the Gift Shop). Due to his support of Sir Wilfrid Laurier's Liberal Party, he was appointed the position of County Registrar.

As the invention of the car was still a few years away, the Bishop family property originally held a large family stable for horses. The stable, which was located at the northwest corner of the property, also served as a storage shed. Unfortunately, this structure did not withstand the test of time and was eventually taken down.

The furniture in the front parlour has been made by the Jacques and Hayes Company of Toronto and is known as "East Lake" style furniture. During the late 19th and early 20th century, the Industrial Revolution was in full swing. As a result of this, all of the furniture made during this era was machine manufactured and mass produced. All of the inlay on the furniture in the front parlour was machine-tooled and is typical of this time period. The notable exception is the green couch, hand-carved in the old "Empire" style, which was handed down through the Bishop family. The rail lines came into Owen Sound in the 1870s allowing for furniture and other goods to be transported to the city. This provided the Bishops with a wider variety of choice for decoration and building materials in the house. The tile on the fireplaces was manufactured by the Spode Company and imported from England.

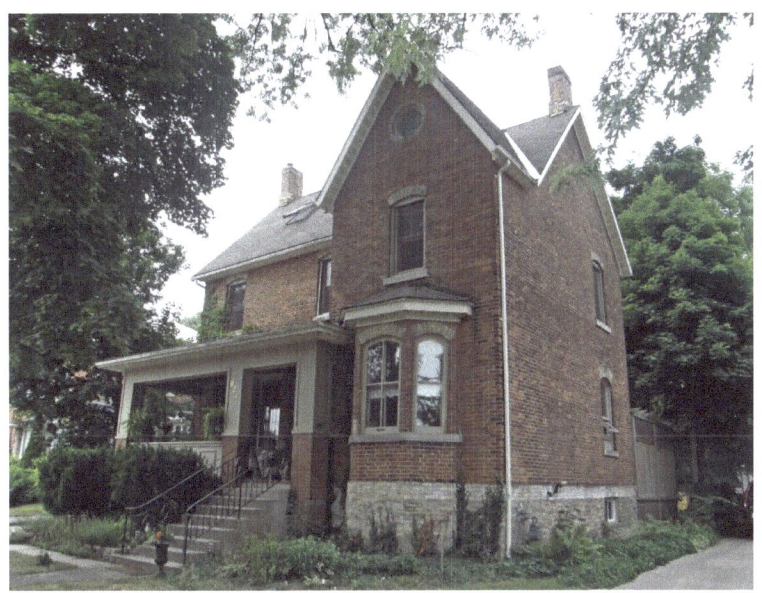

#922 – Gothic Revival, bay window

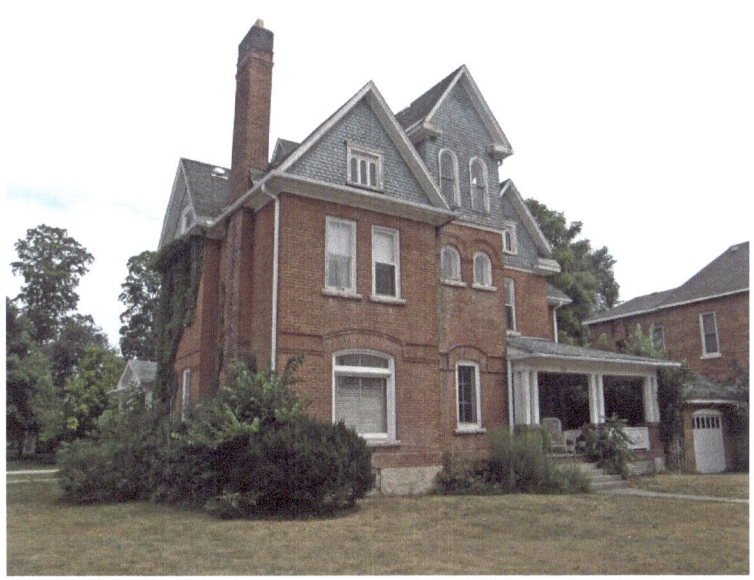

284 9th Street West - Lemon House built in 1891 – Victorian style – vestibule tower, irregular plan and mix of gables, turrets and corners

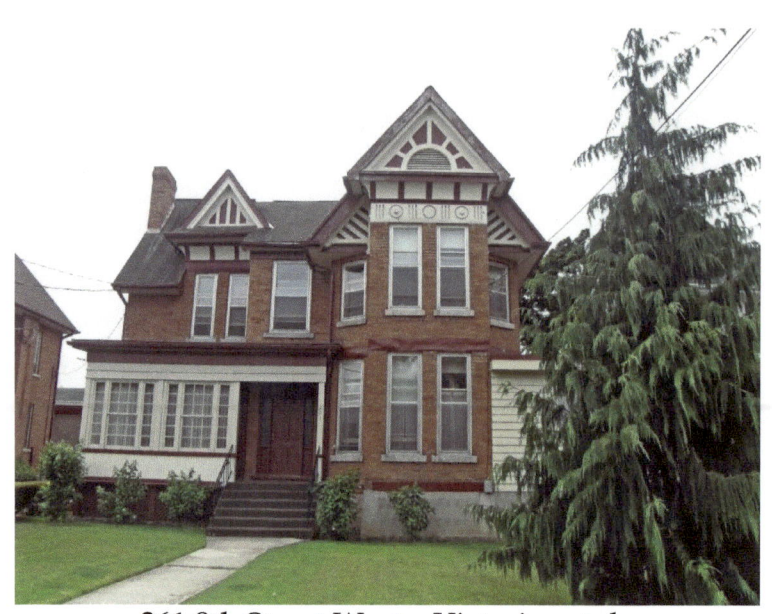

261 9th Street West – Victorian style

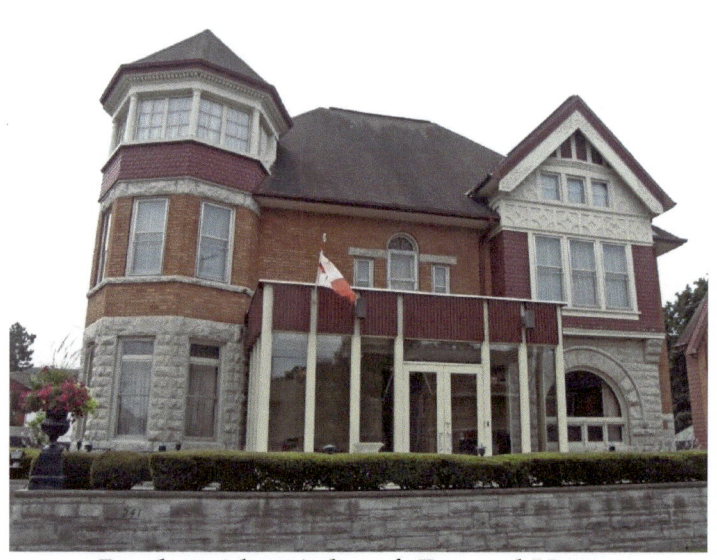

Breckenridge-Ashcroft Funeral Home
241 9th Street West

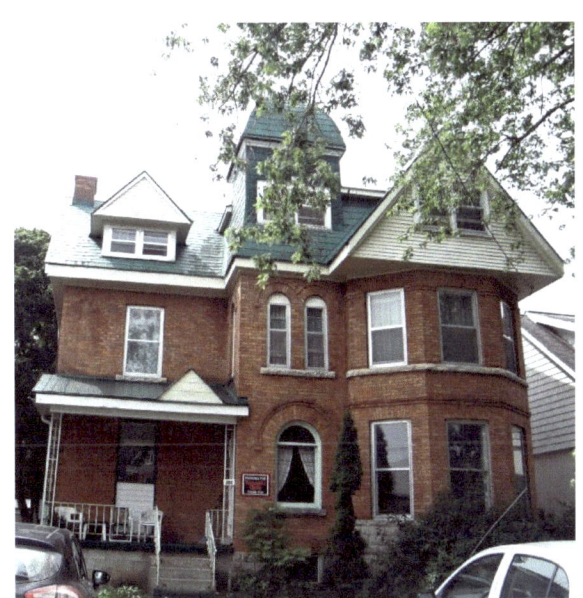

#281 – Vernacular – tower, dormer

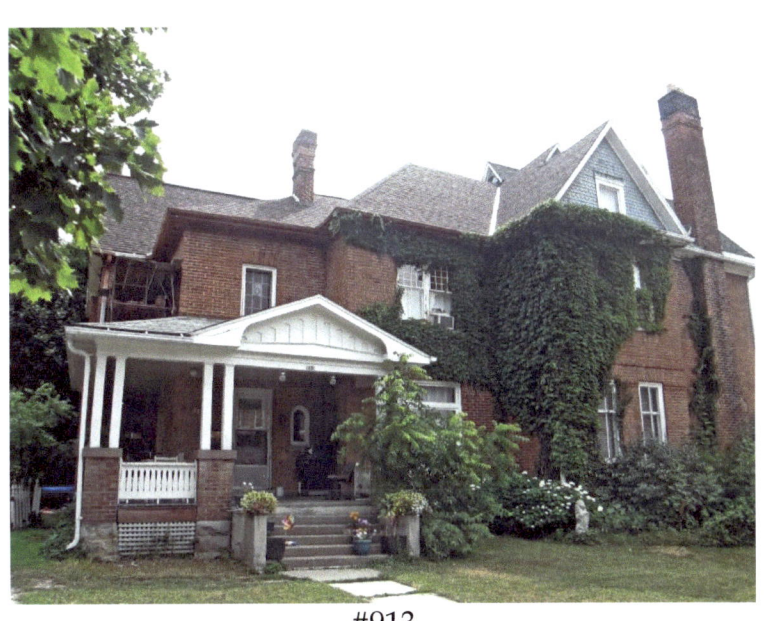

#913

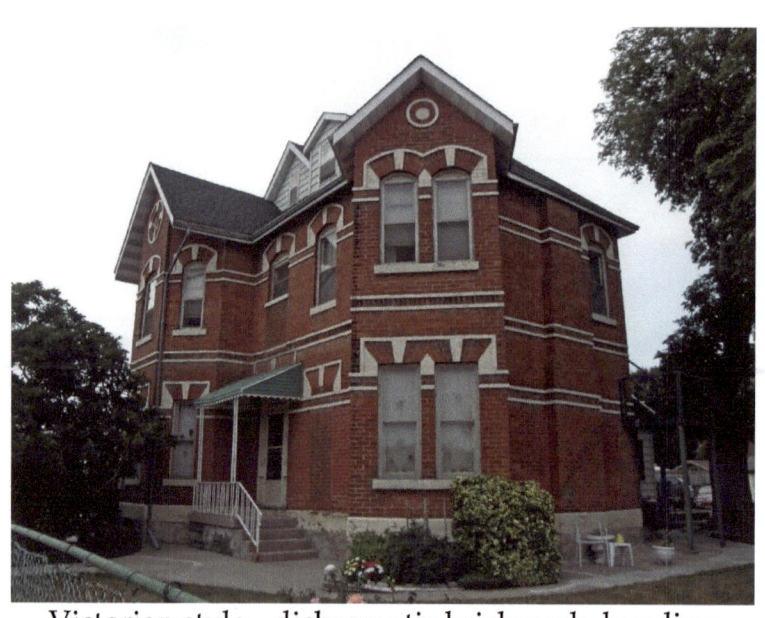

Victorian style - dichromatic brickwork, banding

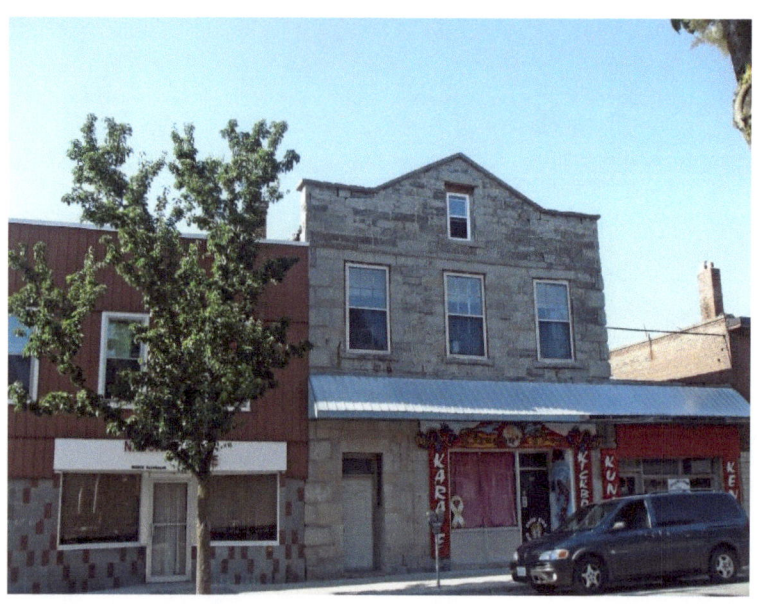

Stone quarries have been an important Grey County industry for over a century. Stone farmhouses, mills, churches, court houses and town halls were made from the local stone. Many of these buildings were built by Scottish and German settlers who brought their masonry skills with them from Europe.

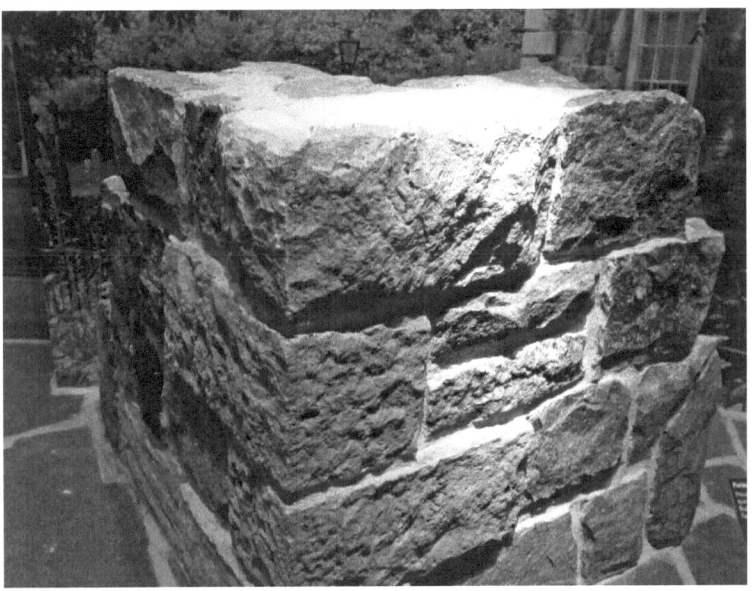

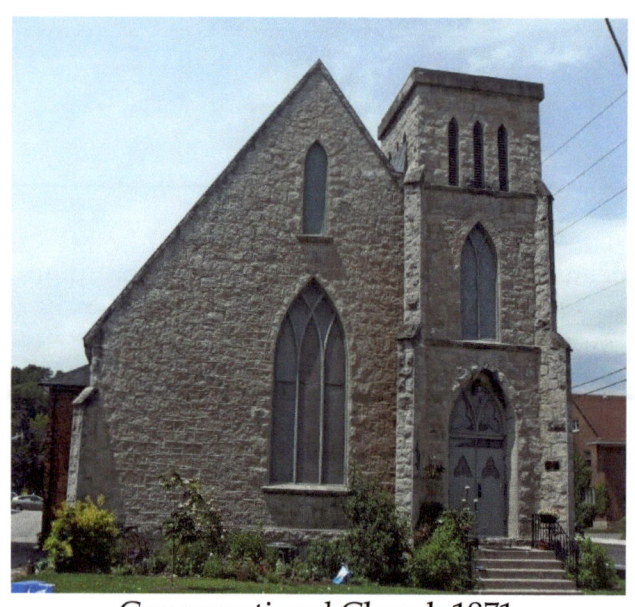

Congregational Church 1871
Women's Christian Temperance Union 1902
Our Saviour Lutheran 1942
Christian Science Society 1963

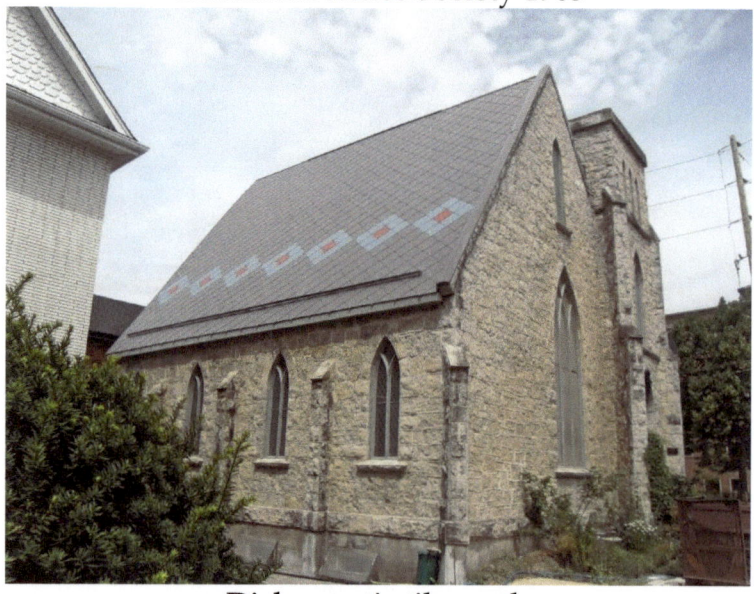

Dichromatic tile work

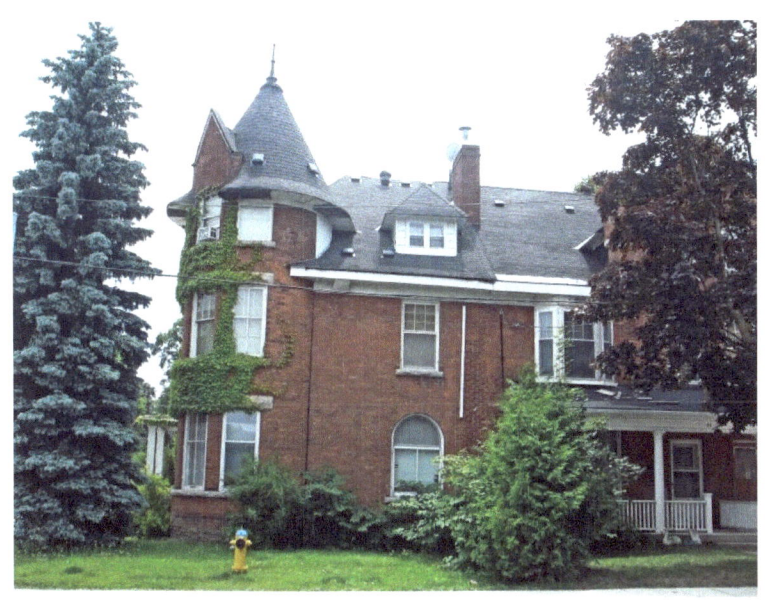

Queen Anne style – turret, dormer

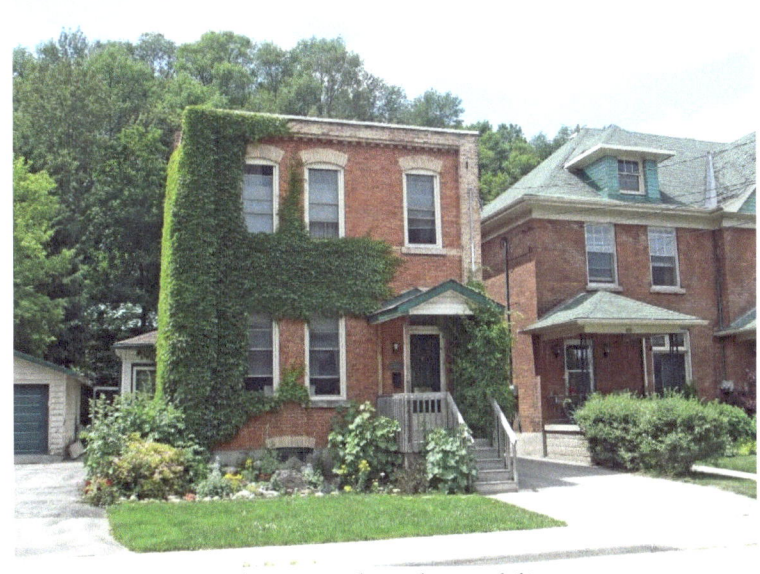

Italianate, dentil moulding

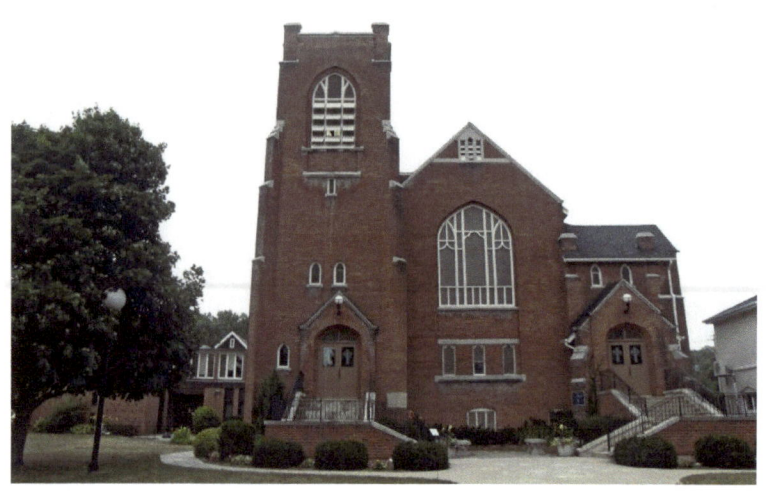

St. Andrews Presbyterian Church, 865 2nd Avenue West
Presbyterianism established in Owen Sound 1845 A.D.
Church corner stone A.D. 1926

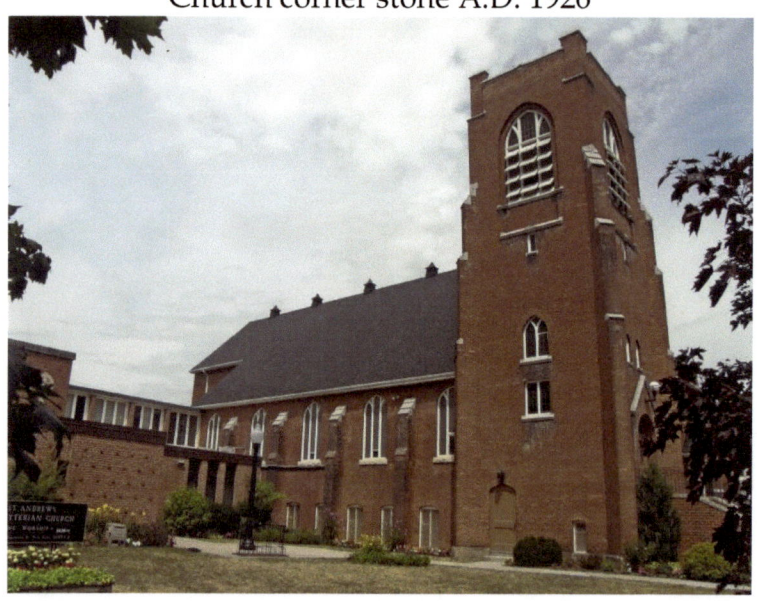

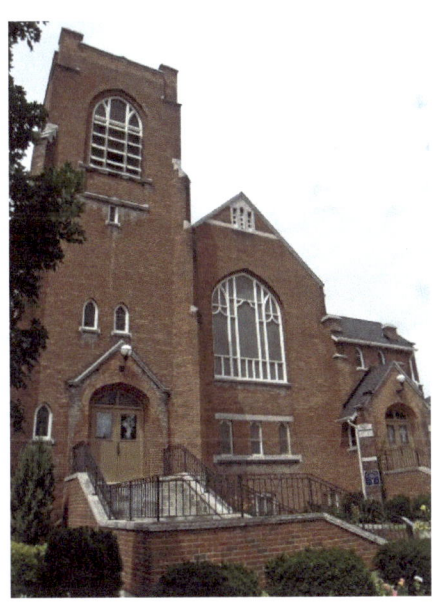

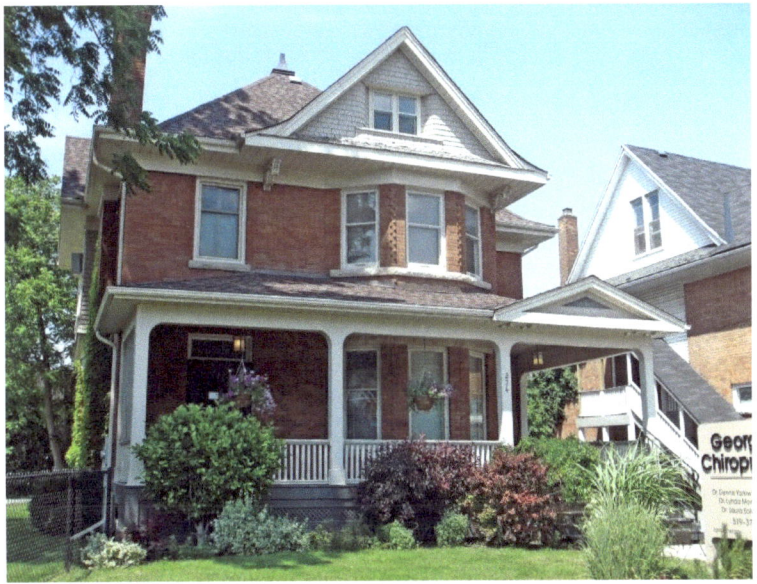

Edwardian

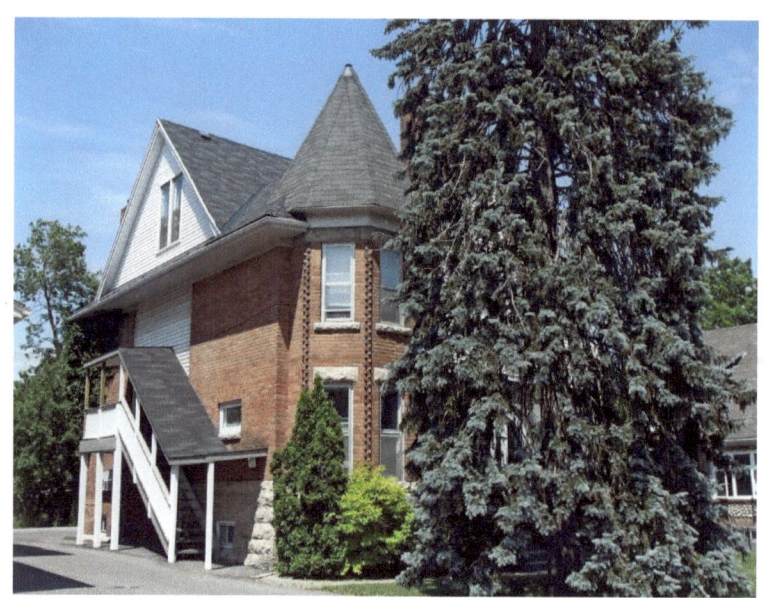

turret

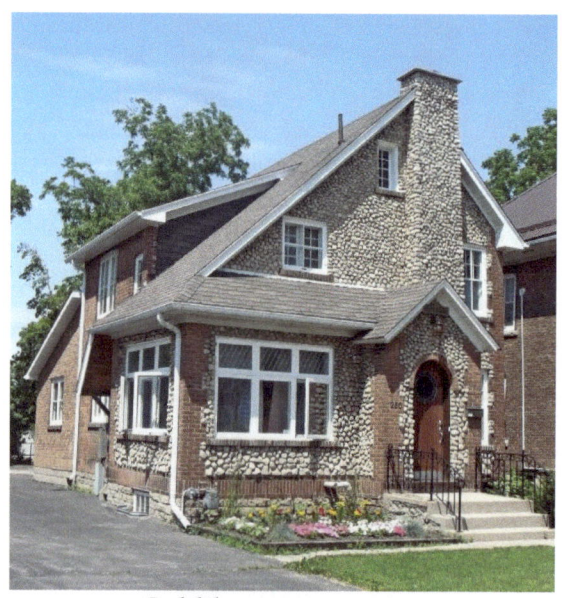

Cobblestone exterior

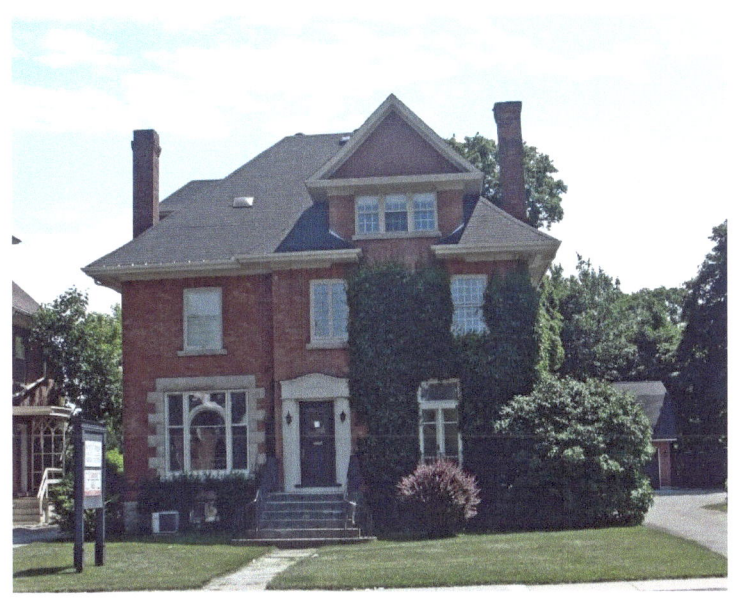

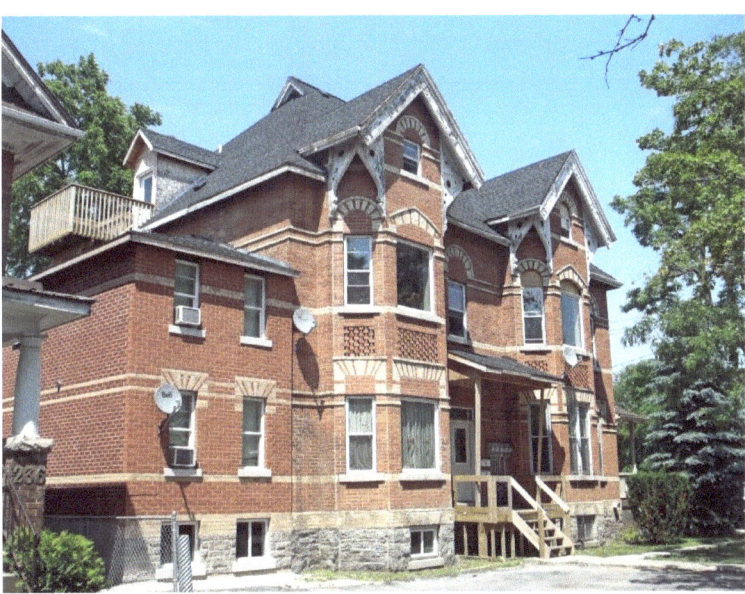

Victorian style – banding, verge board trim on gables, fretwork, dichromatic brickwork

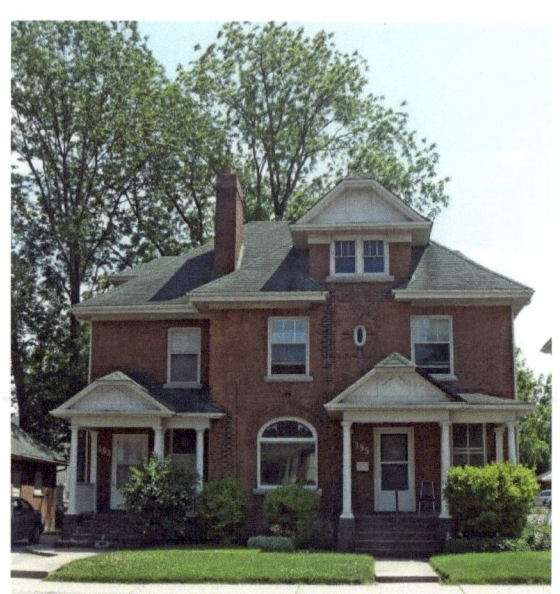

Italianate with hipped roof, 2½ storey tower-like bay,
Pediments above doorways

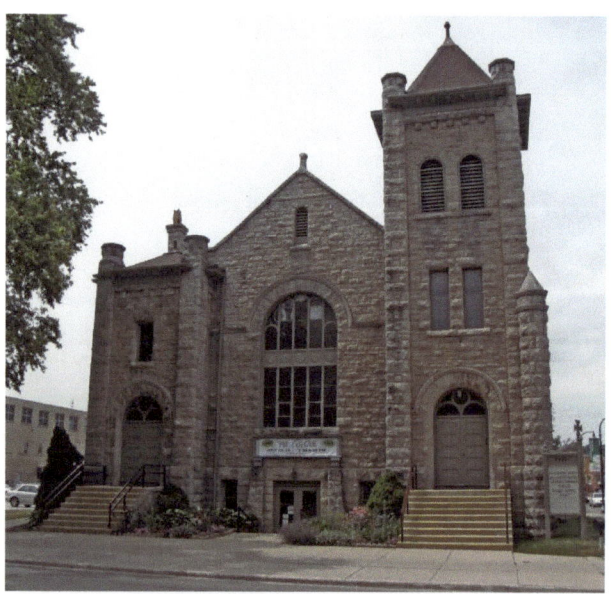

First Baptist Church

The intersection of 10th Street East and 4th Avenue East has a limestone church on each of the four corners.

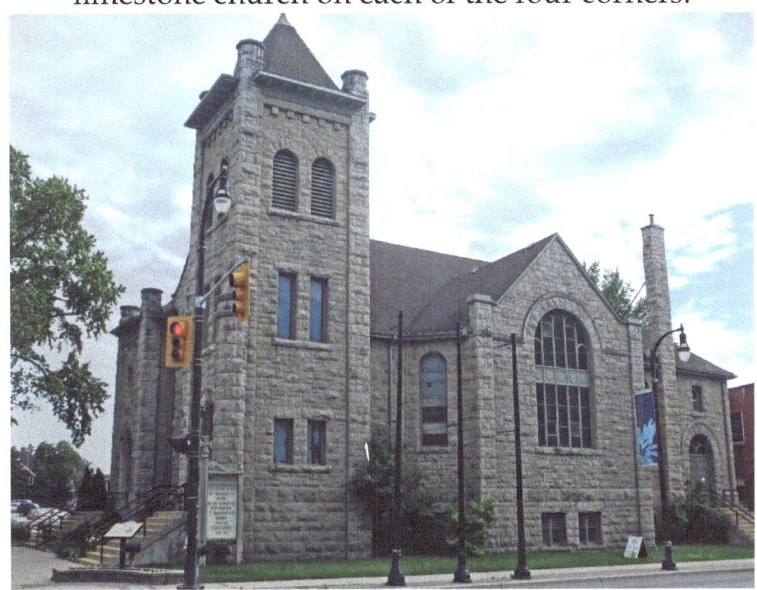

First Baptist Church – stone church built in 1903. The semi-elliptical windows are characteristic of the Italianate style. Square corner towers have octagonal caps.

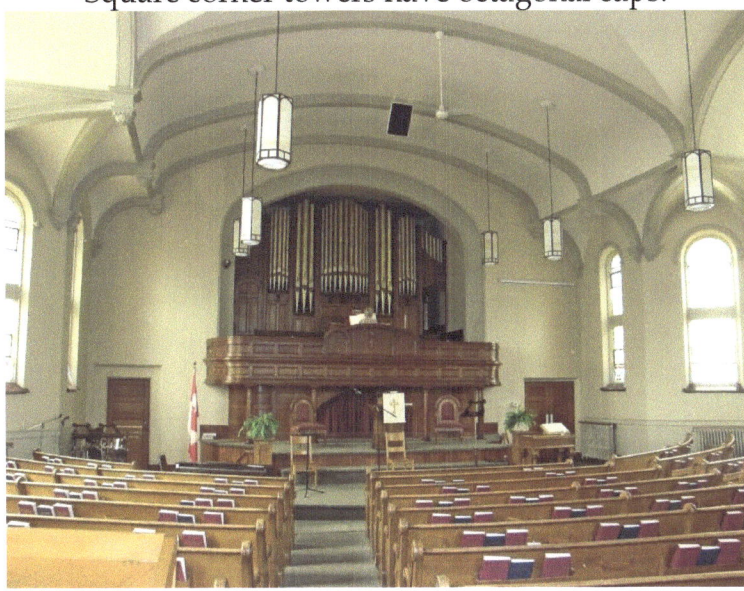

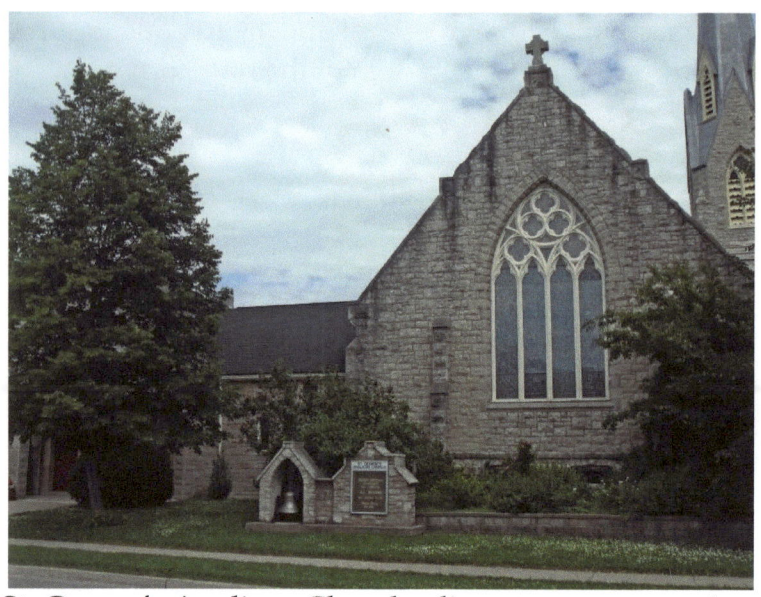

St. George's Anglican Church – limestone construction, opened in 1881, enlarged in 1968, patterned after St. Mary's Church, Bristol, England, in Gothic design – exterior window glazing and quatrefoil (like a four leaf clover), patterned stonework, stepped buttresses

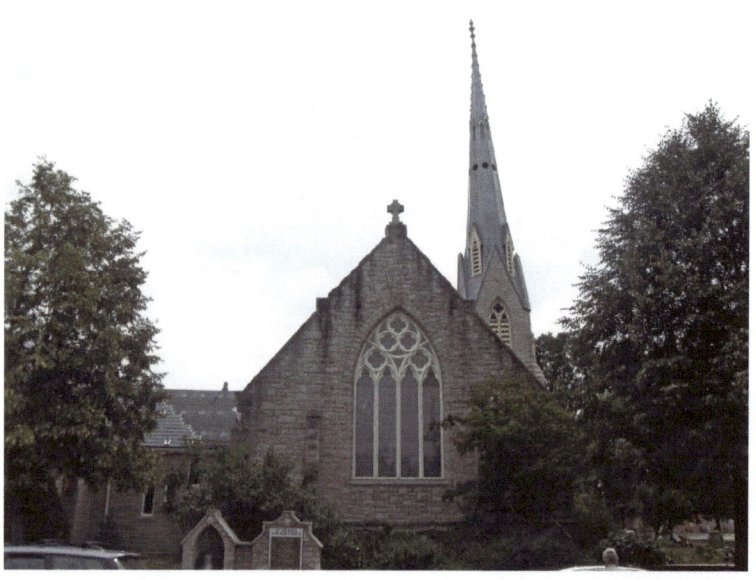

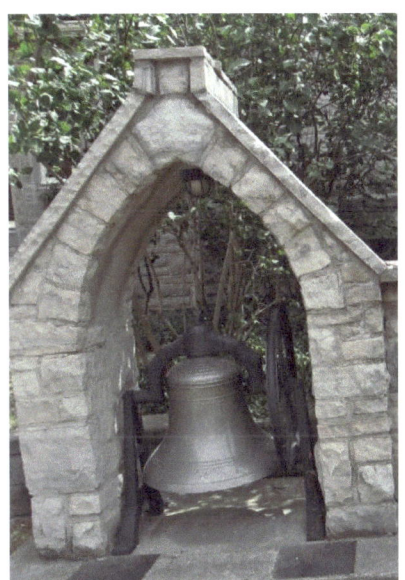

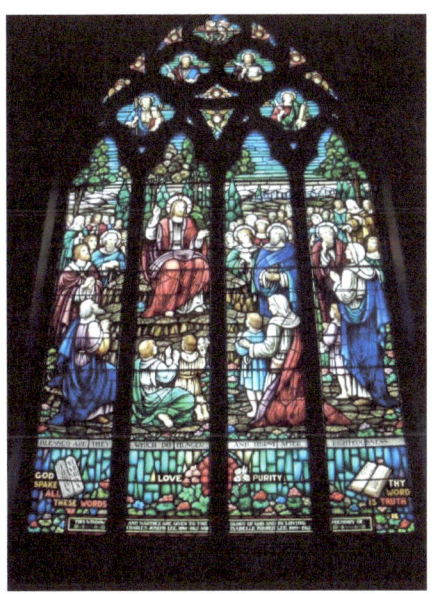

Inside St. George's Anglican Church

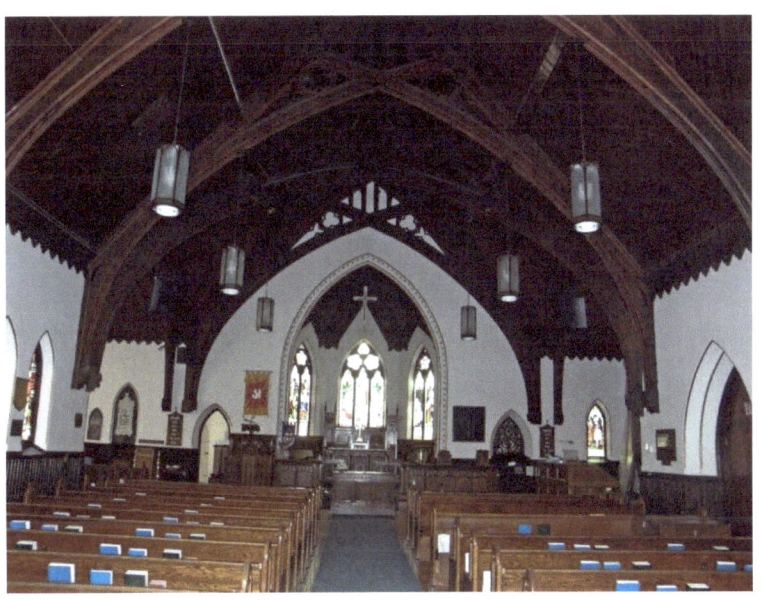

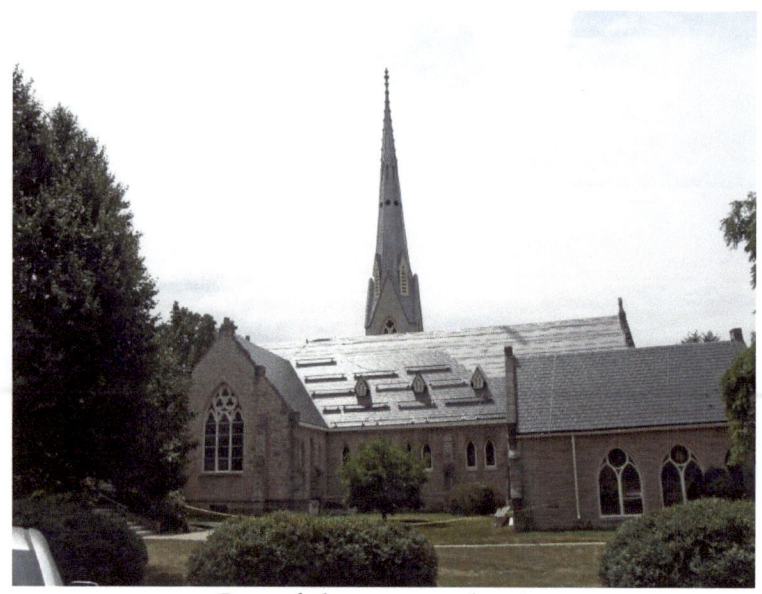

Graceful tower and spire
St. George's Anglican Church

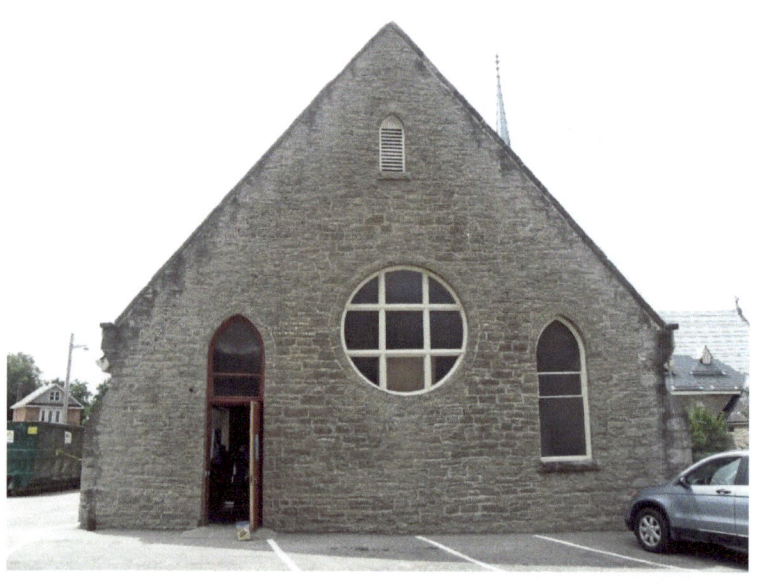

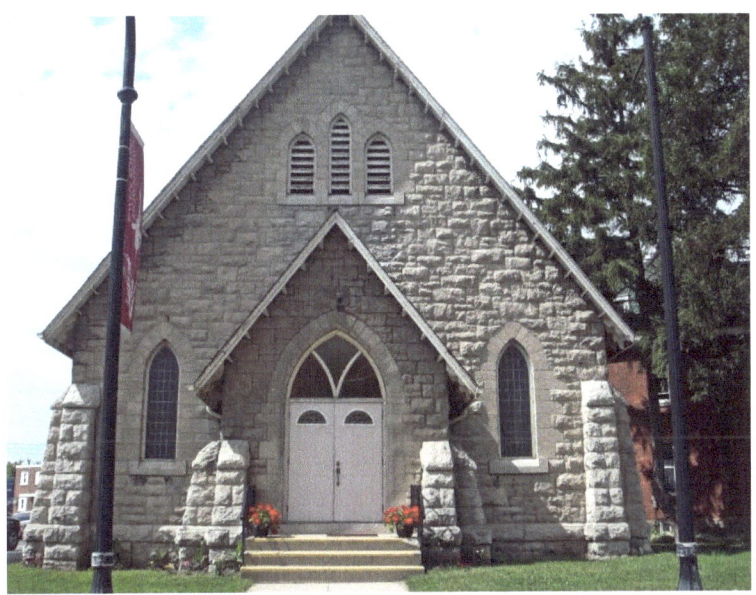

Stone church built by the Church of Christ, Disciples in 1889 in the early English country church style with a steeply pitched roof and sloping buttresses. Gables are cut into roof at the sides with two pointed arch windows. In 1956 this congregation was dissolved. The building was sold to The Church of the Nazarene who continue to use it today.

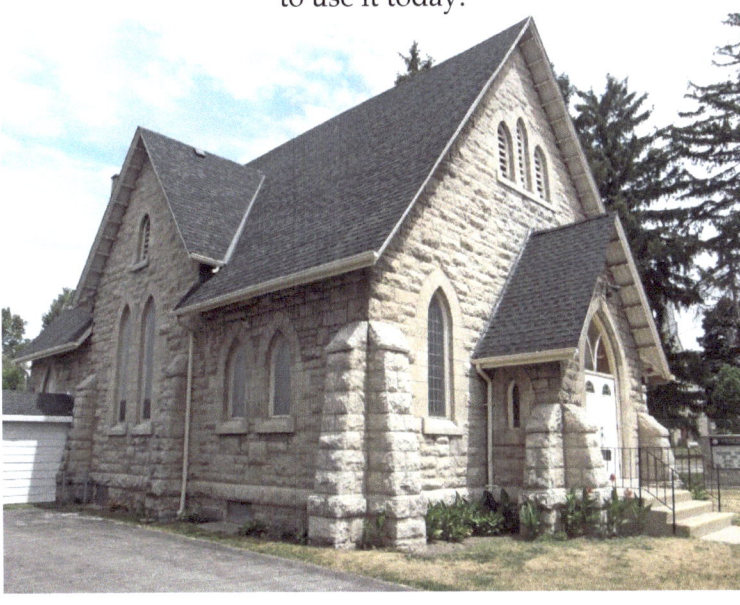

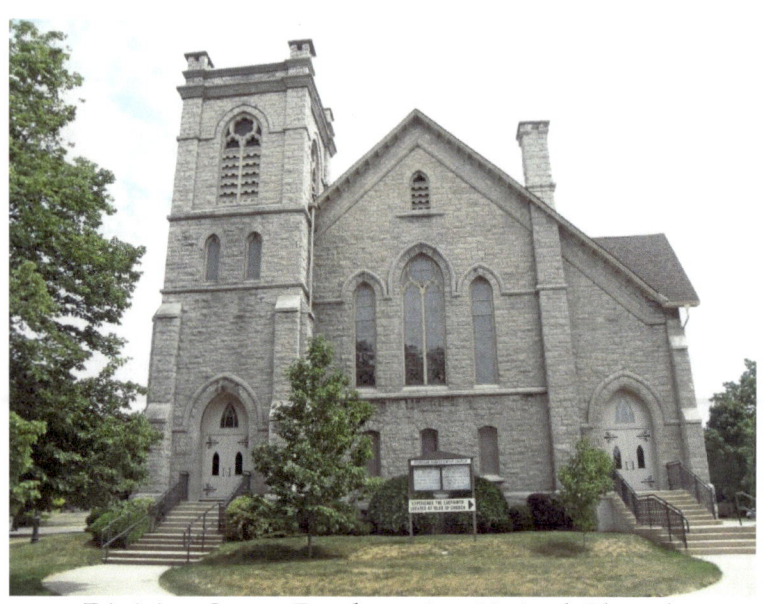

Division Street Presbyterian United Church
Built in 1886 in the Gothic Revival style
The windows are simple openings with pointed stone arches.
There is a square tower and stepped buttresses.

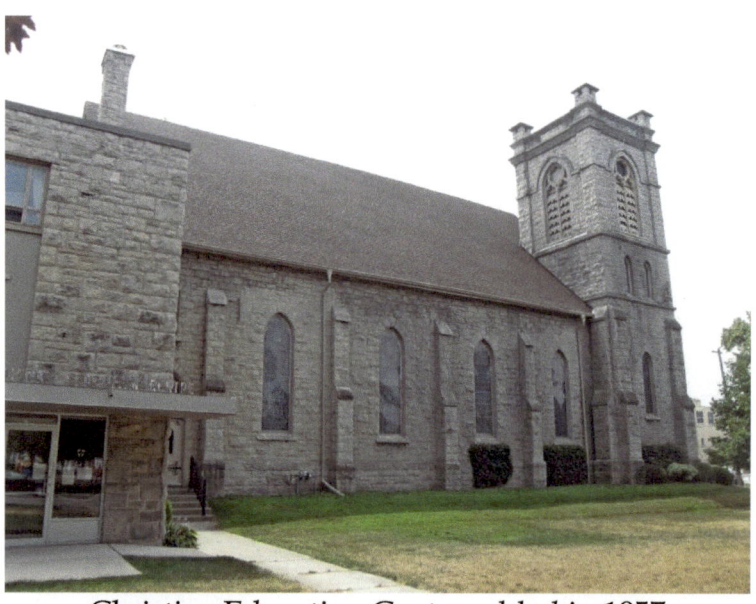

Christian Education Centre added in 1957

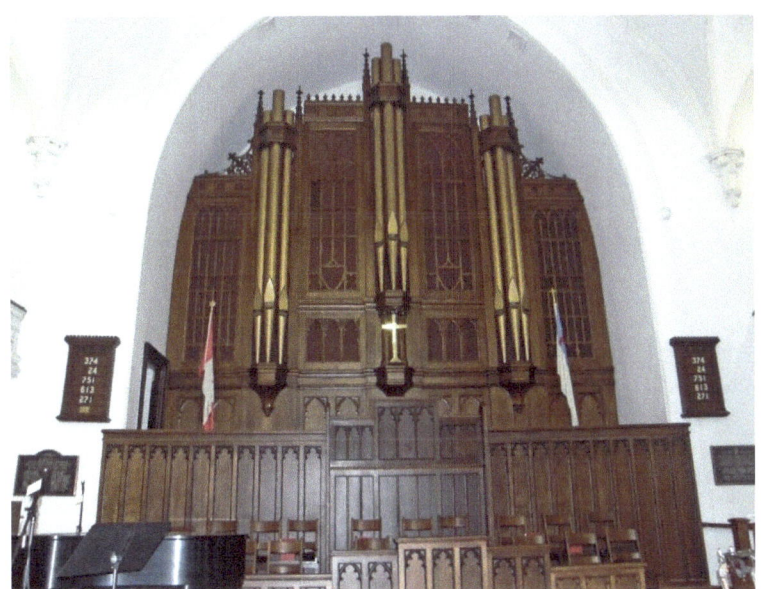

Inside United Church

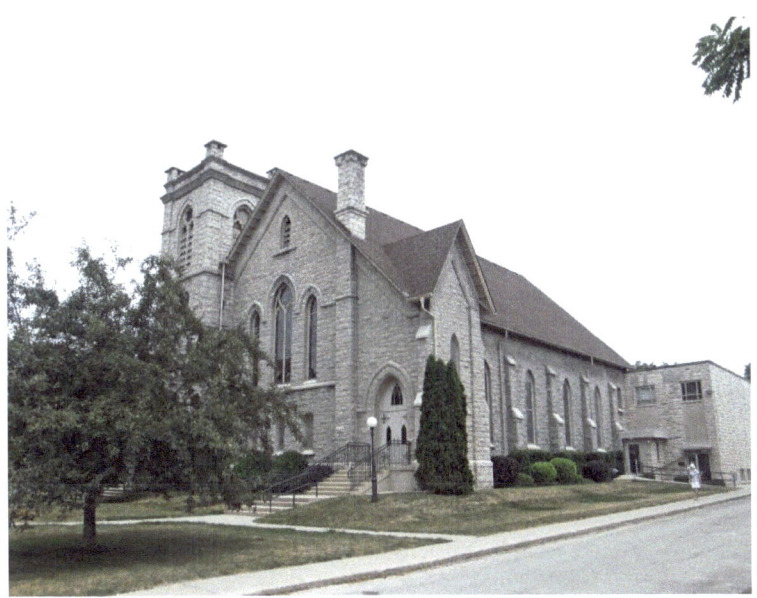

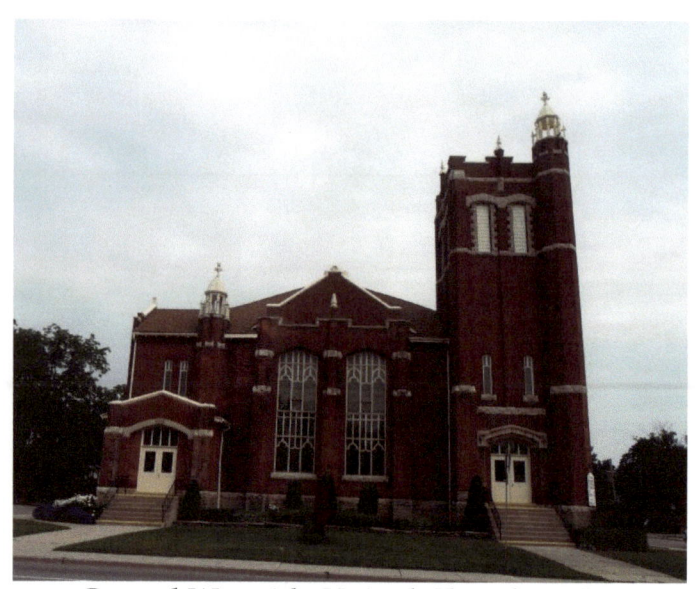

Central Westside United Church – 1910

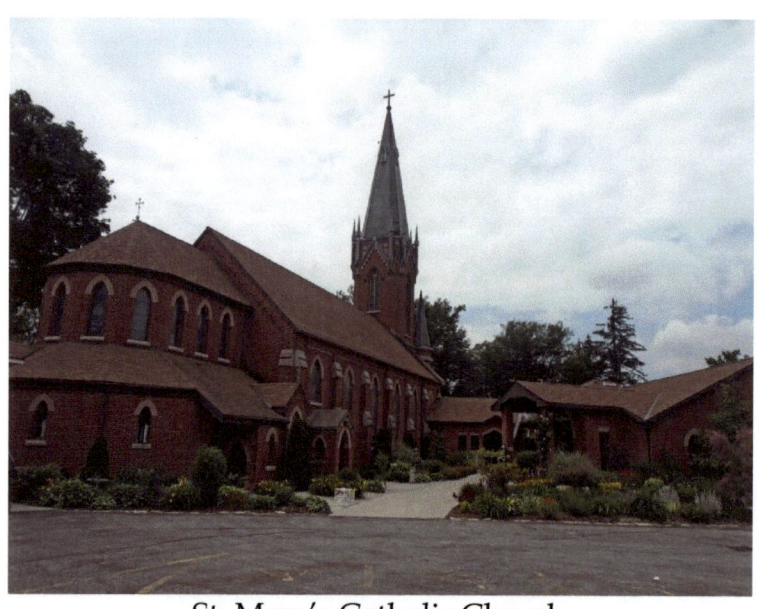

St. Mary's Catholic Church

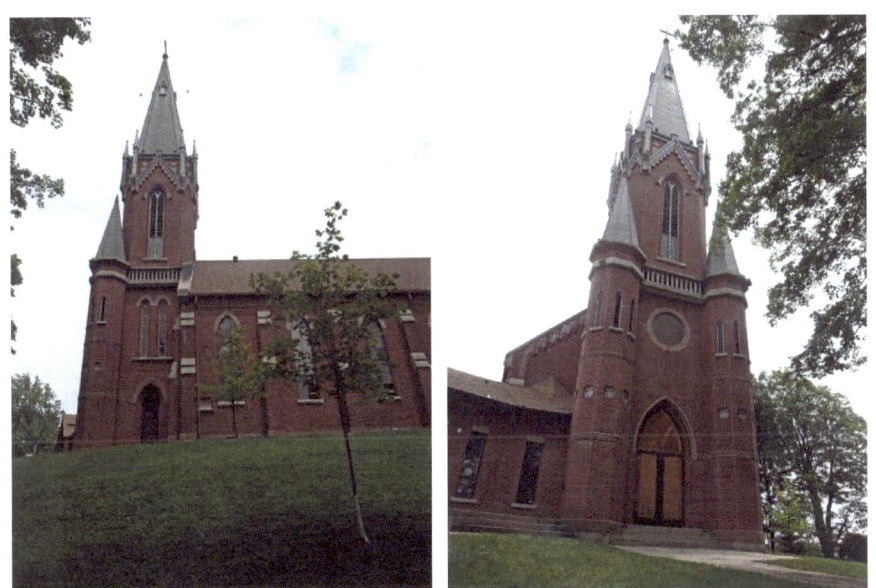

St. Mary's Catholic Church

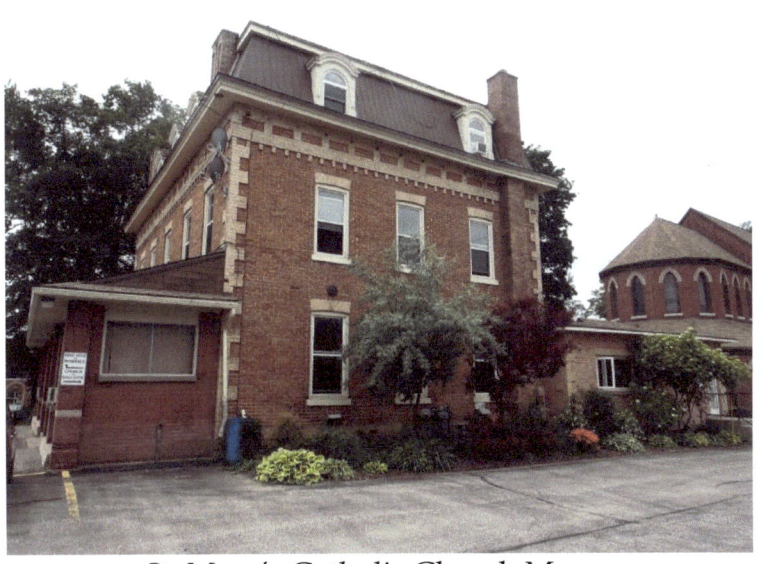

St. Mary's Catholic Church Manse

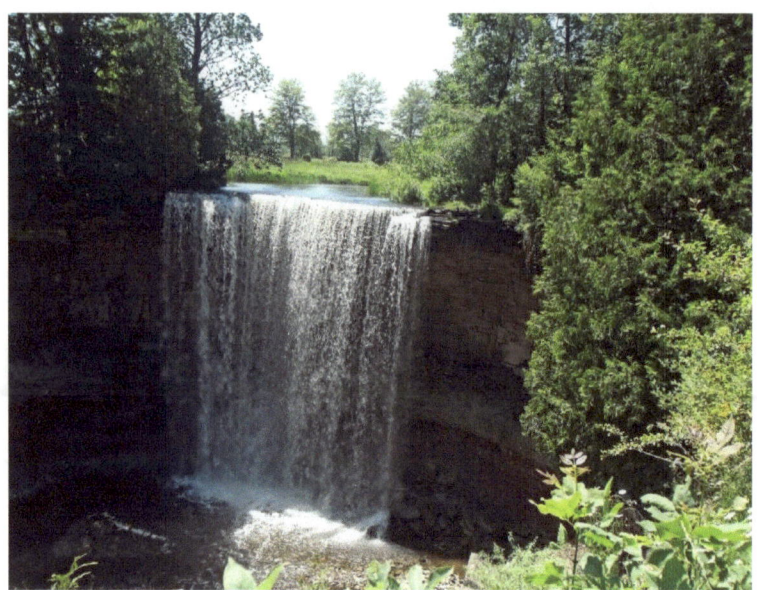

Indian Falls is horseshoe shaped with a "bridal veil" falls. The waterfall drops fifteen metres into an amphitheatre shaped gorge. Indian Falls was formed when the soft red Queenston Formation shale layers eroded exposing the Manitoulin dolomite cap rock.

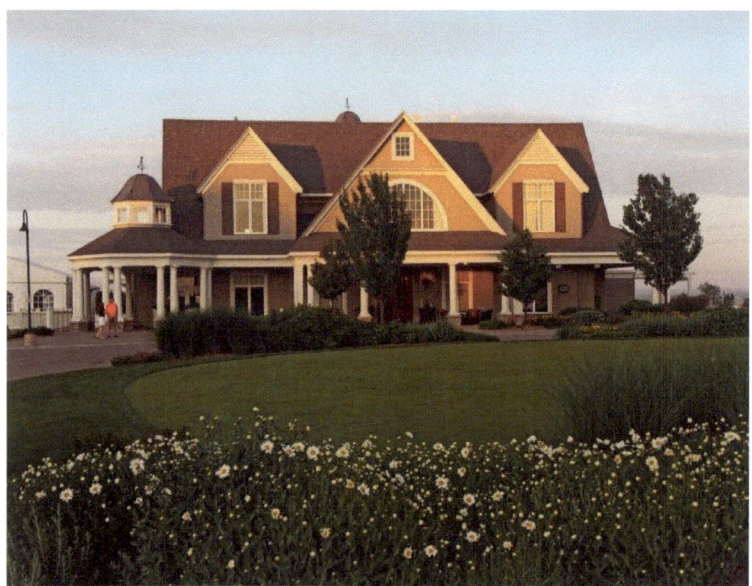

Cobble Beach Resort

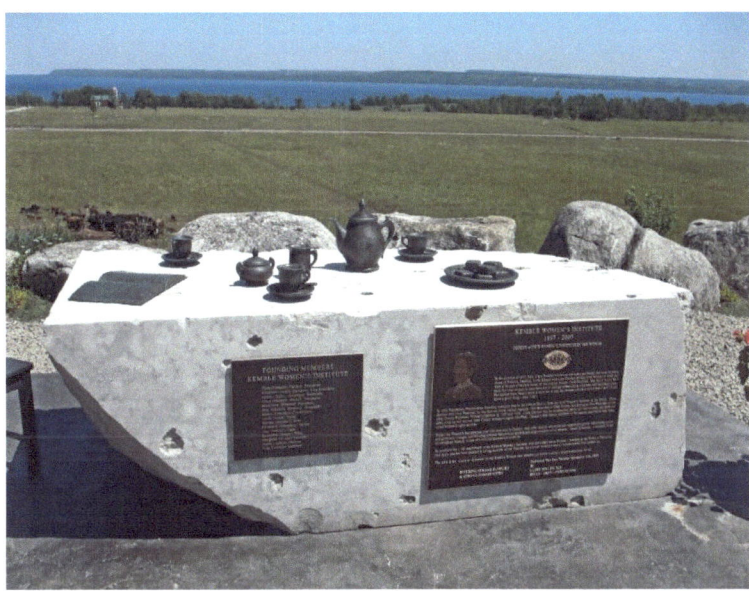

The Kemble Women's Institute Lookout and Teapot Cairn built to honour the world's longest active Women's Institute – provides spectacular scenic views across Georgian Bay to Christian Island. The table is set, tea is ready and there is a book to read.

In the summer of 1897, Mrs. Clara Gardner hitched up her horse and buggy and went house to house in Kemble, Sarawak, North Keppel, and Lake Charles inviting rural women to meet and form a Women's Institute based on the original Stoney Creek Institute. She felt it would be a boon for local women to meet monthly to discuss homemaking problems and exchange ideas. In early September, 23 founding members met to found the third Women's Institute in the world. Clara Gardner was local president for the first ten years, and helped organize other branches in Grey County.

Today, the Women's Institute has over 500 branches in Ontario. Queen Elizabeth, a member of the Sandringham Branch, is one of 9,000,000 members worldwide.

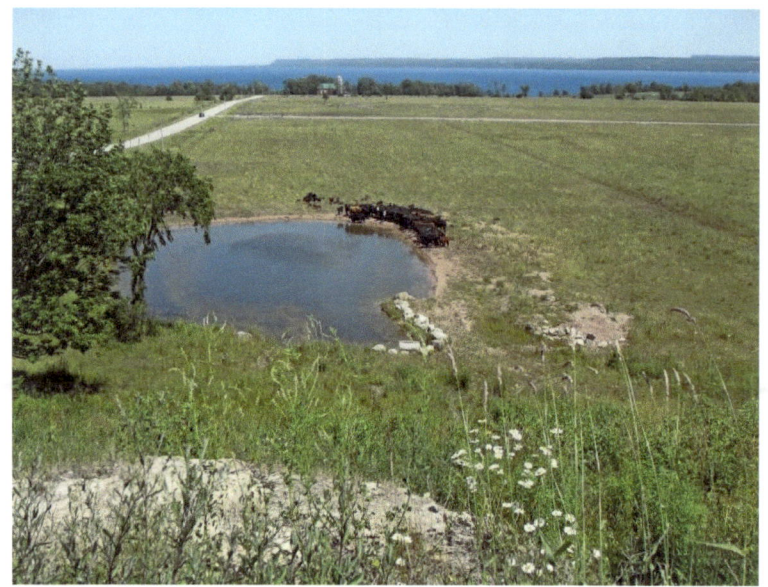

Cattle at the water hole in the valley below with Georgian Bay
in the distance

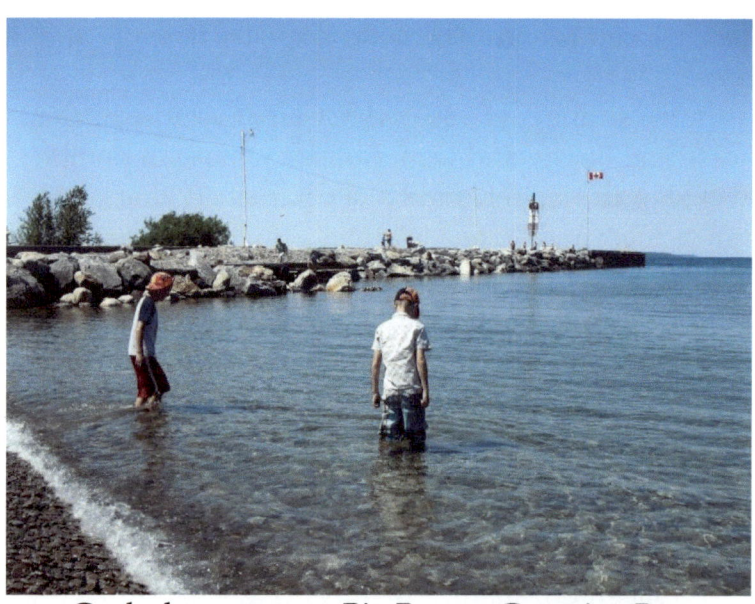

Cool, clear water at Big Bay on Georgian Bay

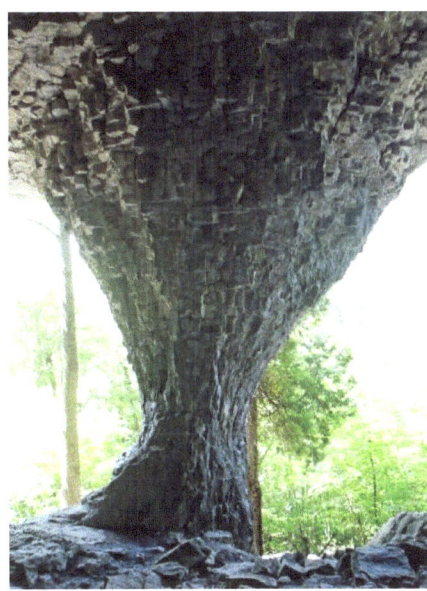

Bruce Caves Conservation Area derives its greatest significance from the unique cave formations found along the escarpment face. These caves were formed by the wave action of post-glacial Lake Algonquin thousands of years ago.

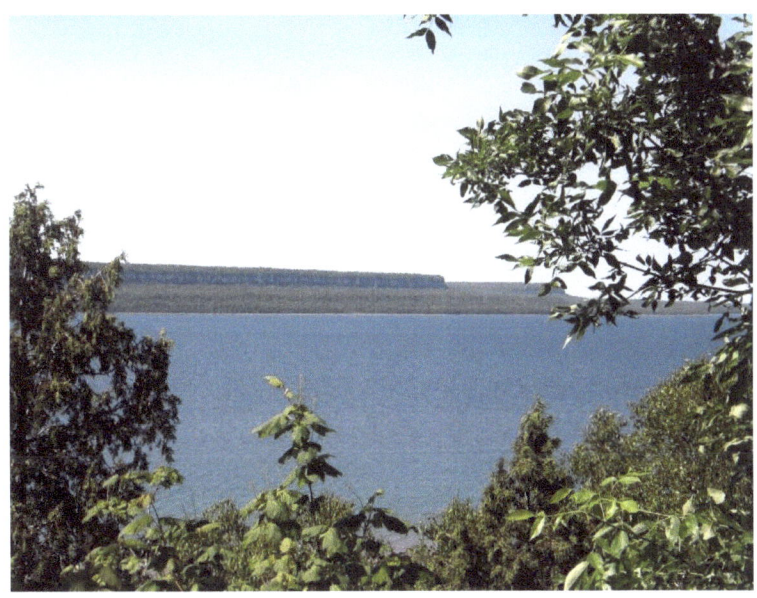

Georgian Bay

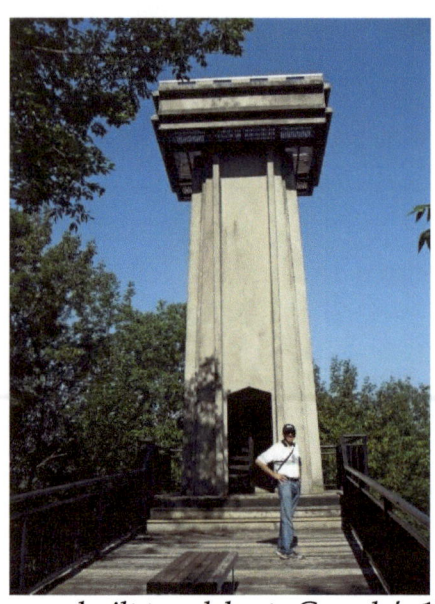

Centennial Tower was built to celebrate Canada's 100th birthday. The tower and the park surrounding it were a joint effort by Owen Sound Collegiate and Vocational Institute and West Hill Secondary School. It was built from funds raised by the students and rises ten metres to the observation deck and overlooks Owen Sound Bay.

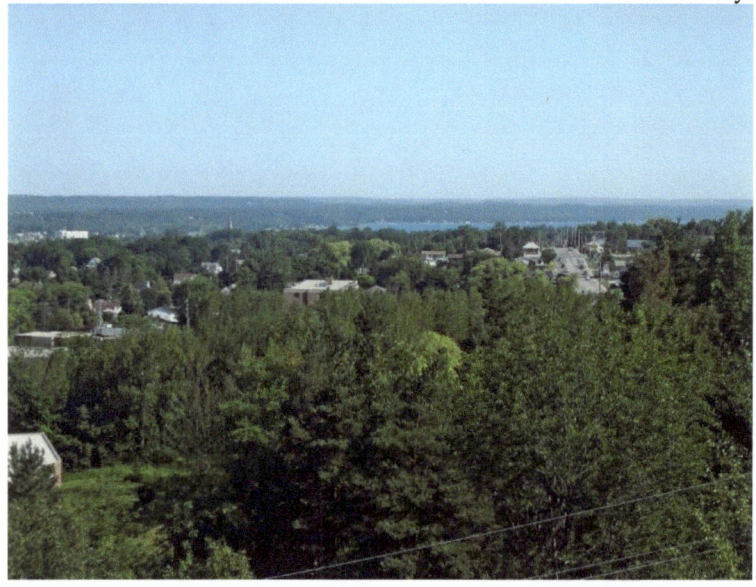

The Centennial Tower is built upon the foundation of a lime kiln and quarry operating on this site since 1887. Kilns processed escarpment limestone for use as building mortar. Portland cement, a product pioneered in Grey County, replaced lime mortar in the construction industry.

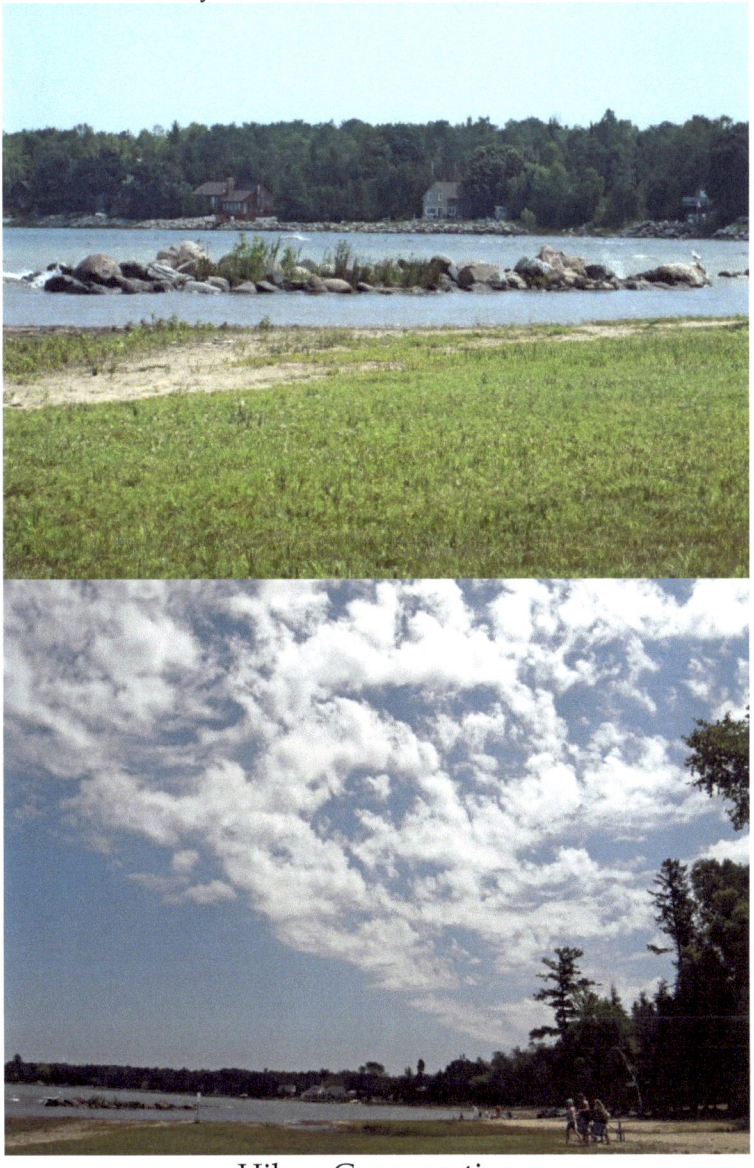

Hibou Conservation

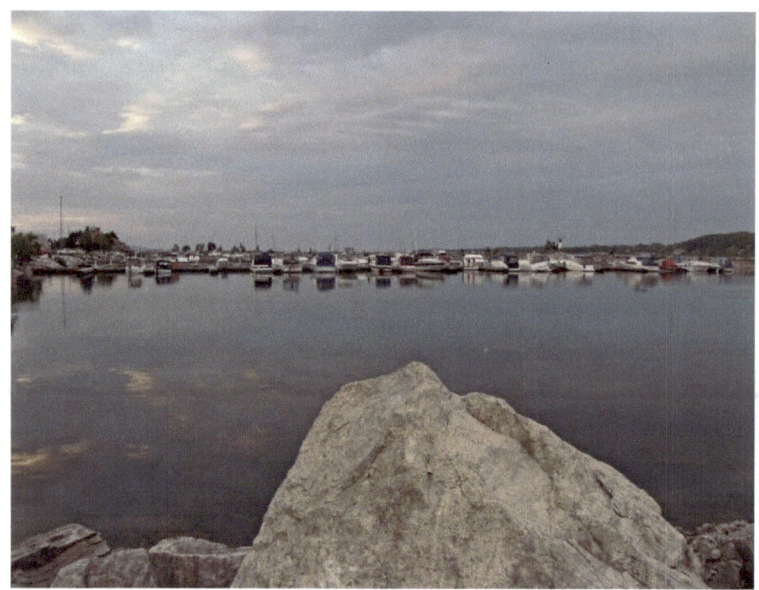

Kelso Beach

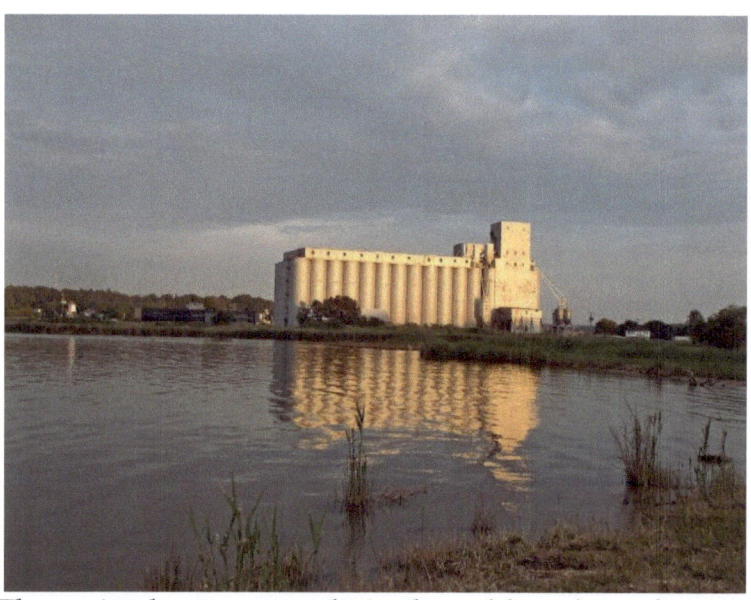

The grain elevators caught in the golden glow of sunset

Architectural Terms

Banding: Different materials, colours or textures used in horizontal bands along a wall. Example: **Example: see Page 38**	
Buttress: a masonry structure built against or projecting from a wall which serves to support or reinforce the wall. In Canadian architecture, they are sometimes used for decoration. Example: Division Street Presbyterian United Church	
Cobblestone architecture: Refers to the use of cobblestones embedded in mortar as a method for erecting walls on houses and commercial buildings. Example: see Page 44	
Cornice: originally the wooden overhang of the roof. With the use of stone, brick, iron and steel, the cornice is any projecting shelf at the top of a ceiling or roof. They can be very decorative. Example: see Page 16	
Dentil Moulding: an even series of rectangles used as ornamental decoration in cornices. Example: see Page 41	
Dichromatic brickwork: the use of two colours of brick, tile or slate to decorate a façade. Example: see Page 45, and 40	

Dormer: (French for "sleep") a gable end window that pierces through the plane of a sloping roof surface to create usable space in the top floor or attic of a building by adding headroom. Example: see Page 24	
Fretwork: interlaced decorative design resembling a bracket Example: see Page 45	
Gable: the triangular portion of a wall between the edges of a sloping roof. Example: see Page 23	
Hipped Roof: a roof where all sides slope downwards to the walls with no gables. Example: see Page 24	
Keystones and Voussoirs: a voussoir is a wedge-shaped element used in building an arch. A keystone is the central stone that locks all the stones into position, allowing the arch to bear weight. A keystone is often enlarged and embellished. Example: see Page 30	
Palladian Window: a large window that is divided into three sections with the centre section larger than the two side sections and usually arched. Example: 1000 First Avenue West	

Pediment: a triangular section above the horizontal structure (entablature), typically supported by columns. The inside of the triangle is called the tympanum. Example: see Page 46	
Pilaster: a slightly projecting column built into or applied to the face of a wall for additional structural support. Example: see Page 30	
Quoin: masonry blocks at the corner of a wall, often a decorative feature, usually larger or of a different colour than the rest of the wall. Example: see Page 18	
Turret: a small tower that projects from the wall of a building. Example: see Page 25	
Verge board and Finial: also called bargeboards – hang from the projecting end of a roof and are often elaborately carved and ornamented. **Finial:** ornament added to the top of a gable, pinnacle, canopy or spire – a Gothic element. Example: see Page 32	

Edwardian, 1900-1930 – This style bridges the ornate and elaborate styles of the Victorian era and the simplified styles of the 20th century. Balanced facades, simple roof lines, dormer windows, large front porches, and smooth brick surfaces are its characteristics. Example: see Page 26	
Gothic Revival, 1830-1890 – These decorative buildings have sharply-pitched gables with highly detailed verge boards, pointed-arch window openings, and dichromatic brickwork. It is a common style in Ontario. Example: see Page 27	
Italianate, 1850-1900 – It has wide-bracketed eaves, belvederes, wrap-around verandahs. Example: see Page 41	
Queen Anne, 1885-1900 – This style is distinguished by an irregular outline featuring a combination of an offset tower, broad gables, projecting two-storey bays, verandahs, multi-sloped roofs, and tall, decorative chimneys. A mixture of brick and wood is common. Windows often have one large single-paned bottom sash and small panes in the upper sash. Example: 948 3rd Avenue West	

Regency Cottage, 1830-1860 – This style originated in England in 1815 and spread to Ontario later in the 19th century as British officers retired to Canada. It is a modest one-storey house with a low-pitched hip roof and has a symmetrical front façade. Example: see Page 19	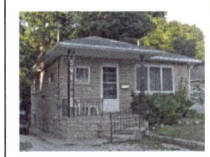
Tudor Revival – exposed timbers with stucco infill, multi-paned windows. Example: see Page 22	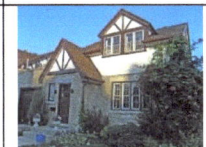
Vernacular architecture is based on local needs, construction materials and reflecting local traditions...a building designed by an amateur without any training in design; the individual will have been guided by a series of conventions built up in his locality, paying little attention to what may be fashionable. The function of the building would be the dominant factor, aesthetic considerations, though present to some small degree, being quite minimal. Local materials would be used as a matter of course, other materials being chosen and imported quite exceptionally. Example: 932 3rd Avenue West	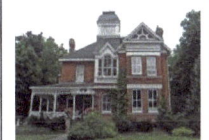
Victorian - In Ontario, a Victorian style building can be seen as any building built between 1840 and 1900 that doesn't fit into any of the aforementioned categories. It encompasses a large group of buildings constructed in brick, stone, and timber, using an eclectic mixture of Classical and Gothic motifs. Example: 284 9th Street West	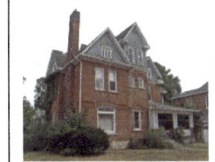